LOUISE MARY SOFAIR was born in Central Africa in 1953 and studied speech and drama in England. She became the principal of a drama studio, also teaching privately at home and abroad. Later she taught at the King's Langley Rudolf Steiner School where she specialised in drama and religion and was active in many aspects of school life, including pastoral care. Having brought up four children, she is now retired but continues to write, study and to support the work of the Christian Community church.

WOMEN WITH CHRIST

Contemplations on the Months of the Year

Twelve Women who Changed the World

Louise Mary Sofair

TEMPLE LODGE

Temple Lodge Publishing Ltd.
Hillside House, The Square
Forest Row, RH18 5ES

www.templelodge.com

First published in English by Temple Lodge Publishing, 2015

A CIP catalogue record for this book is available from the British Library

ISBN 978 1 906999 84 1

Cover by Morgan Creative featuring 'Christ in the House of Martha and
Mary' by Johannes Vermeer
Typeset by DP Photosetting, Neath, West Glamorgan
Printed and bound by 4Edge Ltd., Hertfordshire

Contents

Introduction

Many people today might ask whether there is any reason to write a book about women as, over the last two centuries, the Suffragette and Women's Liberation Movements, several cycles of Feminism and some prominent female personalities have significantly contributed to raising our consciousness about woman's place in society. In most developed countries in the modern world women share equal rights with men to vote, be educated, have job opportunities and equal pay. Women may make their own choices about what they want to study, which life-style or career paths they intend to follow, and where they wish to travel. It is a woman's free choice whether to enter into a committed relationship or to have children.

Nevertheless, the global plight of women has grown perilous in recent decades, particularly in developing countries. The ruthless exploitation of women in the mass manufacturing industries, in domestic slavery, prostitution and enforced drug addiction, as well as violent physical abuse of women in the name of family or marital honour, war and religion, has reached epidemic proportions. We could certainly say that this atrocity against vast numbers of women is now a humanitarian crisis, which requires immediate recognition and practical solutions.

This issue has profound and far reaching significance for humanity as a whole, because in our unconscious psyche the feminine aspect of the human being, in many cultures throughout history, has been regarded as the representative of the human soul. As such, it has either been feared because of its lower nature, or deified because of its archetypal status. A sense of reverence for the soul which promises the highest human development has all but been lost in modern society. Even the religious devotion of the archetypal Mother perhaps does not address the longing of the modern, conscious man or woman to ascend to the level of true humanity, which has as its aspiration the unity of soul and spirit.

A surviving script from the Coptic Gospel literature, the Gnostic *Pistis Sophia*, describes Christ's journey through the spiritual spheres during His Ascension. On His way he meets the female form named Pistis Sophia who, as representative of the human soul, is sunk in deep sorrow. She has fallen from her original spiritual loftiness at the hands of hostile forces, into 'the black depths of imprisonment, suffering and loneliness'[*]. This picture has indeed become an outer reality which the modern media illustrates on a daily basis, showing women caught in cross-fire, attacked for attending lessons, harshly punished and even publicly executed. Moreover, the inner reality for the soul of all human beings is generally just as bleak, because our materialistic society threatens to expunge all traces of spirituality from our consciousness, leaving even the most 'privileged' people suffering from depths of loneliness and feelings of hopelessness.

The Representative Human Soul, the Pistis Sophia, recognizes that her only true salvation comes from the being of Christ. In the Gnostic text, He teaches her certain prayers, which will help her ascend to enlightenment and a redemption of her rightful place in the highest spiritual spheres. Perhaps, therefore, we should try to access the aid

---

[*] See *The Three Years* by Emil Bock.

which the Christ Being offers us, in order to attain the salvation which the human soul is searching.

One of the ways of receiving Christ's help is through the contemplation of particular events in the Gospels and how these relate to the rhythms of the Christian Year. It is generally recognized that there are high points or festive moments in the year, particularly at Christmas and Easter. There are other important seasons: Advent, Epiphany, Lent, Ascension and Whitsun, St John's Tide and Michaelmas. In fact, every month of the year is influenced by the life, teaching and presence of Christ and, as the monthly rhythm is innately connected with the feminine form, this book features twelve monthly contemplative chapters, focusing on the women mentioned in the Gospels.

Since Christ was incarnated on Earth, certain women have played an important role in the development of the Christianized human soul. This book attempts to recognize those women who furthered Christ's work on earth during the second millennium. Of course, many more women could be mentioned than the dozen explored in the second part of this book.

Human beings have a tremendously hopeful future if they can only find their way to a unity with the Christ and therefore with their higher ego. The unity of soul with its spiritual self is the 'marriage' which is expressed in countless fairy-tale endings and myths, as well as in the Apocalypse. Women have the potential to lead the way forward through their sense of devotion, inner striving and an understanding of that world which is not subject to material sense reality. Otherwise, mankind's obsession with that which is earthly will ultimately be death-like, both to the soul and to the world.

This book, of course, is not meant to be read only by women. It is hoped that everyone will take an interest in the particular focus of the subject-matter. The journey through the pages of this book has, as its destination, the positive future of all humanity.

Part One

CONTEMPLATIONS ON THE MONTHS OF THE YEAR

JANUARY

And when they saw the star they were filled with exceedingly great joy. They entered the house and beheld the child and Mary his mother, and they fell down and worshipped him . . .

When Herod realized that it was futile to expect the priest-kings to return to him, his rage flared up. He ordered that all the boys who had been born in the last two years in Bethlehem and the surrounding area be killed . . .

Matthew 2: 10, 11, 16

Presentation of the Child Mary (fragment), Titian

A Matriarchal or Patriarchal Society?

While many women today enjoy an equality of status, freedom and opportunity in the sphere of learning and work, we continue to live in a largely patriarchal society where there are many blatant atrocities committed against female citizens of the world. Yet we cannot return to the type of matriarchal society within which humanity was once harboured, having now outgrown the 'dreaminess' of that state and developed, since Christ's incarnation on earth, a civilization which is the expression of the individual. A change from the matriarchal ordering of life can be discerned in the narrative of the New Testament — but we also perceive the way in which Christ worked as part of this transition and beyond, preparing us for a new society which can best support the human being as a conscious ego-being, with balanced feminine and masculine soul attributes.

The Gospel according to Matthew begins by proclaiming that Jesus Christ became a man and cites the patriarchal line from which he was descended, although a few women are also mentioned. While various patriarchs are quoted as having 'awakened [their sons] to life', of Joseph it is said that he was simply 'the husband of Mary'. It was to Joseph that an angelic being appeared in a dream, who told him that Mary had conceived through the power of the Holy Spirit. Joseph obeyed his spiritual intuition, married Mary, named the child Jesus and later fled with his family to Egypt during the night, in order to save his son's life. He remained in Egypt until he had another dream-vision of the angel and understood that he could return safely with

his family to Israel. He knew where they should specifi-
cally settle once he had received further inspiration from
the spiritual world. In Jesus' father we perceive a morally-
developed man who devoted his actions in life to an
obedience of his intuition and to the advice of the elders
within the high Jewish religious order.

Mary also courageously and unquestioningly did all that
was demanded of her. Matthew describes how, juxtaposed
with Mary and Joseph's modest sense of deep responsibility, some priest-kings from the East made a journey to
Jerusalem to find the newly born, prophesied 'King of the
Jews', according to their astrological insight. They knelt
down, both to worship the child and in reverence of Mary,
the most honoured woman in all of history. This Mary was
a mature, highly developed soul, whom her elderly parents
and the leaders of the Temple had nurtured (she was given
to serve in the Temple as a young child). They knew that
she was 'the Promised One' who would bear the expected
king of the pure Jewish bloodline.

The priest-kings were, like Joseph, capable of spiritual
intuition. They also experienced a dream-vision which
they obeyed and accordingly, after their visit to Bethlehem,
did not return to King Herod, who was waiting, avari-
ciously, for them.

In Herod we see a different sort of man—one who had
attained the political power to rule the Roman territory of
Judea. His subjugation of the people under his jurisdiction
was so oppressive that he was able to order, with impunity,
the massacre of all the infant boys who had been born in
the area within a certain date. Herod knew that this action
would not affect the female bloodline of the Jewish people
but was terrified that an individual male Jew would pose a
threat to his position. At a time when matriarchal power

had been usurped by masculine rule, as epitomized by the Roman Empire, such men as Herod enforced their power through aggressive, even violent methods or through legislation and bureaucracy. Sadly, we still see too much evidence of such things, even in our world today, when a more balanced, intuitive and humane attitude should have the upper hand in the leadership of nations around the world.

A new era had been ushered in at the time when Jesus was born; one where logic, reasoning, organization, rule-making and the development of intellectual thinking had taken precedence over the creative, intuitive, emotional and nurturing psyche. The ultimate conclusion when this, albeit necessary consciousness, becomes one-sided is witnessed today in wars, a lack of equality between rich and poor around the world, the acceleration of a dependence on technical products, the dangers of global pollution and the extinction of plants and animals due to commercial greed.

We can read in the gospels that Christ was never admonishing or forceful towards the women with whom he came into contact. So at the marriage at Cana he asked his mother: 'Woman, what have I to do with thee?' Mary passed the ritualistic celebration-act over to Him, by instructing the servants to 'do as he says'. This transference of the 'feminine' rites over to the 'masculine' resulted ultimately in the transformation of water into wine — an exceptionally high act whereby the life-stream of the earth (known as Mother Earth and inherited from the previous Moon Evolution[*]) was metamorphosed, through the power of the new, sun-filled, life forces of Christ.

---

[*] See *Occult Science* by Rudolf Steiner.

Christ nevertheless revisited the subject of women being treated as equals, after Cana. For example, he challenged the elders to throw the first stone at the adulteress and chastised the disciples for upbraiding Mary Magdalene, who had anointed him with expensive oil. The last few words he spoke from the cross were to his mother Mary and his disciple John, both of whom he considered with equal love and care, willing that John should be regarded henceforth as Mary's son and she as John's mother.

On 6 January Jesus' Baptism occurred, thirty years after his birth. In the gospel description of the Baptism, Jesus is recognized as a 'king' or as the Son whom God loves. While the Holy Spirit was said to have filled Mary, it was the Spirit of God which hovered over Jesus. The boy who was descended from the kingly line of Abraham and Soloman was now proclaimed as the spiritual king of all God's people.

In John the Baptist we have the last great prophet of the Jewish tradition — of him, Jesus said 'Yes, I tell you: among all who were born of earthly mothers, none is greater than John the Baptist'. Yet, the Baptist was aware that the long-established spiritual legacy of the Jewish people had now to sacrifice itself up to something new. The ritualistic ceremonies often carried out by women had to give way to new religious practices, dedicated to worshipping the most highly developed Being of the spiritual Sun-sphere, who incarnated in a human vessel on earth.

January marks the beginning of the year according to the Roman calendar, with its months named after Roman emperors. The sun-calendar usurped the lunar-calendar of Jewish tradition and this is a strong indication that the ancient matriarchal consciousness of humanity underwent a change. In our own time we are faced with the important psychological transition in human beings where both feminine and masculine consciousness must work together in balance and wisdom. In this new mode of consciousness, Christ can live anew and work effectively into human affairs.

The creative Force of the Creator God is a whole world in itself, a Being, which is known as the Word. Over aeons of time preparation was made for the Word to incarnate into the earthly world as the Christ, who provides the Revelation of our present time, teaching us that in the future the division of the human soul from the spirit, as well as the contrast between the sexes into male and female — with many accompanying ills, loneliness and conflicts — will be healed. Through the mediation of Christ, God the Father (the primal Creator-being) and the Holy Spirit (the driving Force which ensures the ordered development of creation) are united. Due to the cohesiveness of this highest spiritual Trinity, humanity can be centred in a continuous stream which connects its past, present and future. The human being will have the opportunity to attain a renewed wholeness and regain its royal position as the 'crown of all creation'.

In the Russian tradition it is Mother Babushka who brings presents to children on 6 January, to atone for having missed the opportunity to travel with the priest-kings to see the new-born Jesus child. As modern adults, neither should we miss any opportunity to devote ourselves to the birth of the spirit within us, nor to recognize a similar striving in our companions.

In January we can be inspired by paintings which depict Mary crowned as the Queen of Heaven, and acknowledge our own wiser, higher nature which may govern our lives and deeds throughout the year.

FEBRUARY

Then came the days of purification as prescribed by the Law of Moses. And the parents brought the child to Jerusalem to consecrate him to the Lord . . .

And see, there was in Jerusalem a man named Simeon. He was devout . . . and he took the child in his arms . . . and said: '. . . Now my eyes have seen . . . a light which leads the peoples of the world to revelation . . .'

And his father and mother were amazed that such words were spoken about him. And Simeon blessed them and said to Mary, his mother: '. . . a sword will pierce your soul, too'.

There was also a prophetess, Anna . . . She never left the Temple and served day and night with inner work on her soul and with prayer. In that hour she also came and offered up her thanks to the heavenly world; and she spoke of the child to all in Jerusalem who lived in expectation of salvation.

Luke 2: 22–38

Head of the Madonna, Andrea del Sarto

Light After Birth

Our thoughts now turn to the Nathan Jesus' mother, the 'younger Mary' as described by Rudolf Steiner in such works as *The Fifth Gospel*. The differences in the genealogical lists at the beginning of the Matthew and Luke gospels are illuminated by spiritual-scientific research, which has brought to light that there was a second Jesus child born to a second Mary and Joseph. This young Nathan family lived in humble obscurity within the Essene community, whose leaders knew that a human being would be required as a pure vessel for the Christ Being, for His entry into earthly life. So the very special Jesus child, having no karma, was born of a mother who was also a pure, young soul. She too was a vessel for a higher being — the original 'world soul of humanity', who was worshipped by all cultures of antiquity as the Mother-Goddess — who came near to the earth in the aura of Mary. She was a member of the divine entourage which accompanied the great process of Christ's coming down to earthly existence.[*] This Mary's whole task in life was to give birth to the Nathan Jesus, to nurture him and to care for him as a young child. It is very moving to perceive, when this Jesus became incorporated by the Soloman Jesus entelechy at the age of twelve and turned away from his parents and home, preferring the Temple, that the young Mary realized her life destiny was complete and that she no longer had a purpose on earth. She faded away and, instead, watched over her offspring from the spiritual

---

[*] See *The Childhood of Jesus* by Emil Bock.

world, remaining close to Jesus and to his adopted mother, the Mary named in the Gospel of Matthew as the mother of the Soloman Jesus (he who had died after he sacrificed his Being to the Nathan Jesus). The broken-hearted young Mary is the archetype of the mother, Herzeleide, in the Parsifal sagas. We may think of her as a Being as pure as the new light at the beginning of the spring season.

In deepest mid-winter the sun imperceptibly begins its ascent towards its highest point in summer. We know that the Jesus child was born at this 'turning point of time' too. In the same way that we cannot readily see the change in the sun's path in the mid-winter period, neither was the birth of Jesus accessible to the world at large. He was born in a humble place, signifying the hidden nature of this special event.

As the sun's presence is generally obscured from us until February, so also was Jesus sheltered from the world until, abiding by custom, his parents took him to the Temple to be consecrated This special 'presentation' was said to occur on 14 February which was forty days after his birth as celebrated in the Eastern orthodox tradition on 6 January. It was only when the Christian calendar was adjusted, making 25 December the celebration of Jesus' birth, that the forty days' presentation in the Temple was said to have occurred on 2 February. This date, coincidently, is mid-way between the middle of winter and the spring equinox and is thought to herald the first signs of spring.

Just as we greet the first spring sun-rays in February, so was 'the Light of the World' greeted by the devout Simeon and Anna the prophetess, in the Temple. This significant moment is sometimes commemorated as 'The Meeting of the Lord' when the two elderly, wise seers foretold of the spiritual enlightenment and salvation which Jesus would one day bring to all people. As the high sun in summer blesses all, so would the light of Jesus Christ bring new life and eventual fruition to all human beings and to the earth itself.

Mary was amazed when she heard this prophecy but contemplated the proclamation about her son in her heart and remained silent. For Mary this was also an important day as, in the Jewish tradition, the day of a child's consecration in the Temple was also the day of ritual purification for the mother who had given birth. So we celebrate 2 February (or 14) as a joint commemoration-day for both Jesus and his mother, Mary.

February had long been a month concerned with the after-effects of childbirth. This tradition was preserved in the Roman festival-calendar as the time of Lupercalia: the cave 'Lupercal' was reportedly the place where Romulus and Remus were suckled by their 'wolf-mother'. It was the custom, during the festival that commemorated this, for men to lash women with soft leather whips, which was said to assist women in giving birth more easily.

According to the Greek myth, the goddess Demeter searched for her daughter Persephone, who had been abducted to the Underworld by Pluto by candlelight in the dim early-spring February mornings. This may have given rise to the relevance of candles at this time of year. Certainly, candles are an important aspect of Christian ritual and are placed on the consecrated altar or in areas of worship. In many Christian churches, 2 February has become the set day to bless the candles which will be used in services during the year to come, giving rise to the name of the festival of Candlemas. One tradition is to process with lighted, blessed candles round the church cemetery, to lighten the after-life for the dead. Some processions enter the church with candles, signifying the Christ-child's entrance into the Temple, when he was acclaimed the 'Light which leads the peoples of the world to revelation'.

In the Gaelic and Celtic traditions, 1 February is the feast day which commemorates the life of St Brigid, who is often referred to as the legendary midwife or, sometimes, as the surrogate mother of Jesus. Brigid is also known as the patron saint of fire and the hearth-side, which is reminiscent of the role of the goddess Vespa, whom the 'vestal virgins' served in Greek and Roman Temples.

It was a long-standing tradition in Western cultures for young girls to be dedicated to temple life in order to serve, particularly in the task of tending the flames which continually burned, signifying the eternal spirit. Christ himself made a reference to this in his parable of the virgins with the oil-lamps. Some of these 'care-takers of the light' were insufficiently prepared. Those who had consciously prepared, however, had sufficient oil — or 'inner light'.

Candles may represent the enlightenment or spiritual purity of a person's inner life. Christ referred to this 'inner light' when he said: 'Therefore take care that the light is not turned into darkness in you. And when your whole body is completely illumined so that there is no room for darkness any longer, then there will be a shining radiance in you, as if a bright light shines within you.' (Luke 11: 35–36). We may think that this is an unreachable goal, almost fantastical to our modern way of thinking. Yet we can be inspired by accounts which describe the end of the life of the individuality of Mary the Mother of Christ, whose body was said to become illumined with a sun-like radiance.

February is a month when we can cultivate inner strength and faith, in order to live through the suffering-time of Lent; knowing that this will ultimately lead to resurrection and new life. The 'light' within us may steadily grow, out of the work and spiritual preparation which we undertake. February is, arguably, the month which lends itself most to the practice of devotional prayer and study.

For Mary the experience of the presentation of Jesus in the Temple was the first moment when she realized that her child, as a very special individuality, would also bring her suffering. Having to live with this knowledge must have been hard for her pure soul to bear and it perhaps contributed to her premature death. The devout Simeon had added that, although her son would cause the fall of many among his people, he would also let them rise again, and even though he would call up dissent, 'through him the thoughts and pondering of many hearts would be revealed'. So can we, like Mary, prepare our hearts for suffering knowing that, through this, Christ brings the fulfilment of our deepest hopes.

The difficult time of Lent and Holy Week, leading up to the events on Golgotha, can be prepared for in February. This can take the form of studying biographies which include the themes of human suffering and death, sacrifice for others and victory over cruelty and adversity. Such narratives or plays, tragic though they may be, should conclude with an element of hope—Shakespeare is the ultimate example of a playwright who fulfills this criteria.

As adults, we may hold up a light for children in our care by keeping their guardian angels in our consciousness. We can also remember in all our contemplations that the Father gave us his Son, to be the Light of our world.

MARCH

In that town there lived a woman who was regarded as a sinner. When she learned that Jesus was a guest in the Pharisee's house, she brought an alabaster vessel of ointment, and standing behind him at his feet she wept and began to wet his feet with her tears and to wipe them with her hair. And she kissed his feet and anointed them with the ointment.

Luke 7: 36–38

A man was ill: Lazarus from Bethany, the home of Mary and her sister Martha. This was the Mary who had anointed the Lord . . .

John 11:1

Then Mary (the sister of Martha in Bethany) took a vessel of precious oil of nard and anointed the feet of Jesus and wiped his feet with her hair . . . Jesus replied [to Judas Iscariot, keeper of the accounts]: 'Leave her be; what she has done shall count on the day of my burial. The poor you always have with you, but you do not always have me.'

John 12: 3–8

The Magdalen Reading, Rogier van der Weyden

'She Has Prepared Me...'

The priest-kings from the East had found the newborn Jesus child, who was destined to be the king of the Jews, and had presented him with myrrh, a very expensive resin which had historically been used in the burial of pharoahs and was usually reserved for kings. Matthew describes how, many years later, a woman 'came up to Jesus with an alabaster jar of the most precious ointment; and she poured it on his head as he sat at table'. It is possible that this substance contained myrrh.

From ancient Egyptian times the anointing of the head was carried out to signify the leadership of a pharoah, and the Jewish people anointed a king's head instead of using a crown. The woman in this instance conferred on Christ his status as king. Christ, however, thought of the anointing as a mark of his destiny, which was one of suffering and death for the sake of all people.

Oil which is used for ritual anointing is often referred to as the 'chrism', from the Greek word *keres*. The name Christ/Khristos means 'the Anointed One'. So, we understand that Christ was already anointed by God and the physical anointing was an earthly act which served as a recognition of that fact. We must ponder whether the woman's inner knowledge was what gave her the courage and confidence to carry out her deed in the face of the disciples, who objected strongly to the use of the ointment. Christ made a point, not only by acknowledging her deed but by saying of the woman: 'Her memory will be honoured' (Matthew 26: 13). So we might conclude that there was a Mystery, a hidden understanding between Himself and (in this instance) the unnamed woman.

There are some Egyptian illustrations of women anointing the feet of their husbands as an act of love. Love is the other aspect of anointing, which is mentioned in two different gospel descriptions. In Luke, a woman who was 'regarded as a sinner' brought an alabaster vessel of ointment to Simon the Pharisee's house and wet Jesus' feet with her tears, wiped them with her hair, kissed them and anointed them with the ointment. Jesus said: 'Her many sins are forgiven her, for she has shown much love.'

St John refers to two anointings in his gospel. When he describes Jesus' visit to the house of Lazarus, Martha and Mary he says: 'This was the Mary who had anointed the Lord with precious ointment and wiped his feet with her hair.' He then goes on to describe a second anointing by Mary: 'Six days before the Passover festival, Jesus went to Bethany ... Martha served at table, and Lazarus was one of those who sat at table with him. Then Mary took a vessel with precious oil of nard and anointed the feet of Jesus and wiped his feet with her hair. And the whole house was filled with the fragrance of the oil' (John 12:1-4). John identifies Judas Iscariot as the disciple who complains about the cost of the ointment, to which Jesus replies: 'Leave her be... The poor you always have with you, but you do not always have me.'

At this time of year, as described in the Gospels, conspiracy, betrayal and plotting against Christ-Jesus' life were taking place. He was aware of this, making it clear in his statement to the disciples that: 'The Son of Man will be betrayed and crucified' (Matthew 26: 2). When he was anointed by the woman in the house of Simon the Leper in Bethany, Christ said: 'By anointing my body she has prepared me for my burial' (Matthew 26: 12). In this way, he was preparing the disciples for his inevitable, fast-approaching death. The day after this anointing, Jesus was hailed as the King of Israel, on the day now known as Palm Sunday. Since then, on Holy Wednesday of Holy Week, the oil used for certain rituals in some Christian churches is blessed for its use throughout the year to come.

In March we experience the greatest dichotomy of the year between the burgeoning of nature around the spring equinox and the period of Lent which focuses on dying, reaching its climax with the death of Christ on Golgotha. We can observe buds, plants and seasonal flowers which continue to unfold, out of an age-old nature force — while we simultaneously remember the end of Christ's life as a man on earth. A new spring can only begin once the old growth-forces have been depleted and died, leaving a seed of renewal. Just as at Michaelmas there is a battle between the summer light and the darkness of encroaching winter, in Lent we come to the crucial point where the old earth-forces have not yet given way to the renewing Christ-force of the earth. The tension between these two great forces brings about a 'crucifixion' of the earth, which was played out by Christ himself on the cross of Golgotha and which we also experience inwardly, either consciously or unconsciously, particularly at this time of year.

It is during the Lenten period that we most need to stay focused on the future resurrection of Christ and, ulti-mately, of the earth. Nevertheless, we must first go through the journey towards Christ's death, whether through prayer, study or religious ritual. It is part of the human condition to experience the dying process, death itself and the turning point towards a new beginning. This happens in Nature during the winter season, leading up to Christmas, but in Lent we need to go through the same process out of our own inner strength.

As an aid to our striving we can contemplate the trials and tribulations of the destiny of Jesus' mother, who saw her first-born son, the heir to the Soloman-David kingly line and the messianic hope of the Jews, die not long after his twelfth birthday. This Mary thereafter experienced her son's soul-nature mysteriously kindled within his friend, the Nathan Jesus, whom she cared for as her own son when the younger Mary and, later, both Josephs died. How much greater was her suffering when Christ Jesus was crucified and all her hopes seemed to have been lost! Nevertheless, she had the soul strength to witness His dying process and she became one of the circle of disciples who experienced the presence of the Resurrected One. Her exceptional destiny was fulfilled when, through the purification of her being, which was won by hard and bitter suffering, Mary essentially became the earthly entelechy of the Holy Spirit, which inspired the first community of Christians at Pentecost.

We read in the gospels how some women, including Mary Magdalene, prepared ointment and aromatic spices to anoint the corpse of Jesus. In John's Gospel, Joseph of Arimathea took down the body and Nicodemus 'brought about a hundred pounds of a mixture of myrrh and aloes', wrapped the body of Jesus in strips of linen soaked in these balsam spices and laid the body in a new tomb in a garden. Then the corpse was subsumed by the earth, leaving only the linen strips in which the body had been wrapped. Mary Magdalene saw two angels in shining white garments sitting, one at the head and one at the feet, where the body of Jesus had lain—that is, in the two areas of Jesus' body which had been anointed while he was alive. Perhaps those special places of anointing with precious substances provided an 'entry-point' for the beings of the angelic sphere to appear in the realm of earth.

The 'wise women' of the time, as well as the 'wise men from the East' and men like Joseph of Arimathea and Nicodemus, no doubt knew the secrets of using certain herbs, spices and ointments for new-born babies, the healing of ailments and wounds, for purifying a body for burial and for attaining spiritual insight. Even today, perfumed essences are still referred to as having certain 'notes'. Mozart was said to have written a whole symphony after smelling a rose. The heavenly spheres are more accessible to us through the use of sacred ointments. Incense is another fragrant substance which can be used for purifying the atmosphere, for example during ritual celebrations.

In March we can endeavour to purge and purify all that is old, no longer necessary, or harmful, in order to live in the hope of new possibilities. The women mentioned in the gospels can inspire both men and women of our own age to have the courage to do this.

APRIL

But Mary stood outside before the tomb and wept. And weeping she bends forward into the tomb and sees two angels in shining garments sitting there . . .

She turns and sees Jesus standing, but is not aware that it is Jesus . . . He appears to her to be the gardener . . .

Jesus says to her, 'Mary!' And again she turns and says to him in Hebrew 'Rabboni'; that means: 'Master'.

John 20: 11–16

Christ Taking Leave of His Mother, Albrecht Altdorfer

The Resurrection of the Soul

After the winter months the first, almost imperceptible sign that the spring season is beginning is the gradual increase of daylight. Birds seem to sense this before human beings. They begin their dawn chorus earlier and we hear the crescendo of birdsong, long before we see the first buds appearing on the branches which had seemed dead, or out of the earth which had seemed cold and barren.

On a microscale, the Gospel describes a similar process in Mary Magdalene's experience of the Resurrected Christ. The first thing that Mary saw when she looked in the tomb where the body of Christ had lain was light: the shining light of two angels (John 20:12). According to the Gospel of John, Mary then heard Jesus' voice asking her why she was weeping and whom she was seeking. When she heard Jesus say her name she recognized him — she then saw, not the gardener she supposed him to be, but the living being of Christ Jesus, who had been crucified. New life had miraculously sprung from the dead wood of the cross and out of the grave of the earth.

In the natural world around us in spring:

> We experience the *movement* of plants, as they grow.
> We observe plants *taking nutrition* from sunlight and water.
> We enjoy nature's *abundance* as every living thing flourishes.
> We feel a satisfaction of our *senses* of sight and touch in the plant world.

After Christ appeared to Mary, He then manifested:

> Walking alongside the disciples on the way to
> Emmaus — *movement*
> Eating ('a piece of broiled fish', Luke 24:43) — *taking
> nutrition*
> Harvesting fish in the sea of Tiberias — *abundance*
> Satisfying the *senses* of sight and of touch (ref.
> 'doubting Thomas')

So we can observe, through the Gospel accounts, that the same force of life which manifests in nature in spring was manifested by the life forces of Christ after He resurrected from death. The stages of this manifestation are:

> Light
> Sound
> Sight
> Movement
> Taking in nutrition
> Abundance
> Satisfying the senses.

Christ's physical body had indeed died and been subsumed by the earth into an earthquake fissure, but His life-force was able to use His former physical body as a blueprint in order to manifest as a resurrected body.

The 'woman who was regarded as a sinner' (Luke 7), of whom Jesus said 'Her many sins are forgiven her' and Mary Magdalene, whom Jesus 'freed from seven demons' (Luke 8 and Mark 16:9) are often assumed to be one and the same person. In all the Gospel accounts, Mary of Magdalene was present with the other women who saw the stone rolled away from the mouth of Jesus' tomb. They witnessed the angelic beings who proclaimed that Christ had risen and who urged the women to tell this to the other disciples.

We know from the Gospel according to John (20) that after the two disciples had seen the empty tomb and left, Mary Magdalene stood outside the tomb and heard Jesus' first resurrection words, thinking him to be the gardener. Mark also writes in his Gospel that 'He appeared first to Mary of Magdalene'. Something of a mystery is at work when a woman of 'many sins', or a woman who was at one time possessed by 'seven demons', should be the first to recognize the resurrected Christ.

The 'sinful' woman of the Gospel, with her last vestige of faith and probably all her money, bought expensive ointment and demonstrated an act of love for Jesus. He recognized her great deed. Through total forgiveness and acceptance He resurrected her true, virginal soul from its death-throes. A soul which had experienced such a resurrection was receptive to the resurrection of another soul, even one which had been through the physical process of death. Because Mary's soul had undergone a resurrection granted by Christ Himself, the core of her being was pure. She was receptive after Christ's death because of her great love for Him. This was the prerequisite soul state for perceiving the newly risen Christ who appeared and spoke to her.

In some cultures, we still hear today that a woman who is raped or involved in adultery has the blame put on her. Girls who are forced into prostitution or sold as sex-slaves are, often as not, shunned by society and treated as criminals. Bereft of family, social-acceptance, freedom of movement, health or joy, such women may lose their souls completely. Other women in modern society can also experience a hardening of the soul forces in a fight to achieve independence, in suffering unmeaningful relationships, or succumbing to the pressures of maintaining an image which may belie a true destiny. Yet a 'resurrection of the soul' from such a state of 'soul death' is still possible through Christ.

If we follow the allusions to Mary Magdalene through the Gospels, we can perceive a tremendous development of character. Luke relates how Christ said of Martha's sister 'Mary has chosen well', referring to the fact that Mary sat at His feet and was occupied only with listening to His words. She had progressed from a follower, whose love had been acknowledged and whose sins had been forgiven, to Christ's pupil. Because of the particular relationship between Master and pupil, Christ asked Mary to be present when He performed the act of bringing Lazarus (her brother) to life. Was this a further initiation lesson for Mary, now a pupil, as well as a preparation for her future experience of the Resurrection?

According to Luke, Mary Magdalene was one of several women whom Jesus had healed of evil spirits. From this description it seems that she was not sinful but had been 'possessed' — or, as we now understand, possibly suffering from a mental illness. Such sufferers may hear internal voices other than their own, and this manifests as an illness when these voices induce the person to act unwittingly. It could be that, due to unresolved karmic issues, a 'karmic overlay' of personalities worked on in Mary Magdalene's soul. Either way, Christ restored seven 'beings' to their rightful states, which allowed Mary thereafter to act out of her own free will. Her free, restored soul was then able to 'hear' a higher being than herself : a stage of inspiration.

We can wonder what initiation teaching Christ gave Mary that induced her to anoint Him in preparation for His burial. He told the disciples that 'wherever in the whole world this Gospel is proclaimed, what she has done will be told and her memory will be honoured'. Mary of Magdalene was not called to be a disciple, apostle or priest. She was, rather, 'chosen' — the saying 'many are called but few are chosen' may describe Mary Magdalene as one of the few who were chosen by Christ, the Master.

But what of the other women mentioned in the Gospels who came to Jesus' tomb with aromatic herbs — Joanna, Mary the mother of James, 'the other women who were with them' (Luke 24) and 'Salome' (Mark 6)? When the women told the apostles that the stone had been rolled away from the tomb, 'it seemed to them like empty talk; they did not believe them' (Luke 24). When Mary Magdalene proclaimed to the disciples that she had seen the Resurrected Christ, 'their hearts could not grasp it' (Mark 16).

Nowadays men and women need to use logical, coherent language to describe spiritual experiences. The language of spiritual science is a means by which we can describe the spiritual reality of the universe. Yet Christ manifested in a new way to those who had damaged souls or minds or who were unable to put into words clearly what they had witnessed and experienced. The Gospel women in particular are a 'signifier' to us that in order to see the angelic realm, hear the spiritual Word and know Christ, we do not need to have always been virginal or to have lived a life apart or be intellectually erudite. Rather, it is a question of maturity of the heart, humility and openness of the soul.

Our inner life is greatly enriched when we become aware that the outer, physical manifestations of nature in the month of April are but reflections of the joy of a new 'spring-like' state of being. Mary Magdalene, the epitome of the World Restored-Soul, was the first to experience this joy when she recognized the Being of the 'new-born' Christ.

MAY

In unity of soul they devoted themselves to prayer, together with women and with Mary the mother of Jesus, and with his brothers.

Acts 1: 14

As the time of the fifty days neared its fulfilment they were waiting with shared devotion for the beginning of the Whitsun festival. Then suddenly a sound came from the spiritual heights like the rushing of a mighty wind, and it filled the whole house in which they were gathered. And to their seeing there appeared tongues of fire, like flames which divided until they came to rest on each one of them. And they were filled by the Holy Spirit and began to speak in foreign tongues; each uttered what the Spirit gave him to say.

Acts 2: 1–4

Pentecost, Duccio di Buoninsegna

The Mother

Christ manifested his Resurrection Body through the stages which nature goes through in spring — first through an increase of light, then through sound, movement, taking in nutrition and becoming tangible. Then, in the same way that the seeds of plants are released and become airborne, so the Christ Being freed himself from earth-bound existence and ascended into the airy regions. This was witnessed by the disciples as the Ascension, the time when Christ's forces of life filled the space surrounding the physical earth and all spaces to be found between physical entities; the moment when His life-force spread into and permeated the life force of the earth. He now lives in this sphere, the invisible sphere nearest to us, in which we can find Him in a new way.

Christ gives renewed life to all minerals, plants and creatures on earth. He also endows human beings with this, regardless of whether they perceive or acknowledge the fact. In this sense, we truly are a global community but our consciousness is not always able to fully encompass it. Even in the space weaving between two people in a relationship, the Christ can be found if we try to perceive Him. The consciousness required today to recognize Christ in the world is a necessary factor for the fulfilment of what is known as the Second Coming.

We remember that Mary conceived the Holy Spirit and she shared this experience with a small community consisting of Joseph, Elizabeth, the shepherds, Simeon and Anna. Many years later, this young Mary had died but remained spiritually close to 'the other Mary'. By means of an extremely intense, esoteric conversation, in which Jesus poured out his whole soul to his adopted mother (the other Mary), before sacrificing himself as a vessel for the Christ Being, the spirit of the young Mary was able to unite itself entirely with the now mature, experienced Mary.[*]

Not many days after the disciples witnessed the Ascension, they were gathered together in shared devotion with this 'duality-being' of Mary, when the Holy Spirit came upon all who were present. So, at last, the knowledge of the indwelling of the Holy Spirit, which Mary (notwithstanding her own complex destiny) had kept in her heart throughout Christ's life on earth, could now be shared with a larger community.

Furthermore, the festival of Whitsun was the moment when all the disciples were enabled, through language, to share their experience of the Holy Spirit with many other human beings with whom they came into contact; indeed with people all over the world. Just as one 'flash storm' can cause plants to suddenly sprout abundantly, so this one moment at Whitsun enabled Christ's incarnation and resurrection to become comprehensible to many human beings. We are reminded of Christ's words in the parable of the sower, when He said: 'Lastly, a portion of the seed fell into good earth and grew and bore fruit, a hundred-fold' (Luke 8:8).

The Holy Spirit manifested as a sound like rushing wind, a 'rain' of fire and the ability for each individual to utter what the Spirit gave him to say. We can sense the power of this force, which at the same time manifested as a love for all mankind. The disciples' experience at Whitsun resembled an autumn storm of wind and rain, yet the inner mood

---

[*] See *The Fifth Gospel* by Rudolf Steiner.

was one of warmth and community spirit. This was a 'new autumn' experience.

What the disciples underwent at Ascension had been reminiscent of the height of summer, when human beings are normally exhilarated by the joy of sunshine. The disciples had been inspired because, before He blessed them and vanished from their sight, Christ 'opened their understanding for the scriptures'. They were overjoyed, because they now comprehended that all that had been prophesied had been fulfilled. This 'new summer' experience was filled with the light of certainty.

Whatever the outer conditions during Lent, inwardly it is a quiet, contemplative, 'winter time', when we need to develop a determination to face the demands of earthly destiny. Easter, on the other hand, is very clearly the moment when we experience the overcoming of death-like obstacles by the sun-forces of the living Christ: an 'inner spring'.

So Lent gives us hopeful will-forces, Easter gives us healthy life-forces, Ascension gives us enlightened astral-forces, and Whitsun gives us the warmth of loving ego-forces.

These 'new seasons' can thus be associated as follows:

> Lent — inner winter
> Easter — inner spring
> Ascension — inner summer
> Whitsun — inner autumn

Most of these festivals occur in May, as the beginning of May often falls within the Eastertide season; Ascension Day and Whitsun are always celebrated in May.

Although May is not the middle month of the twelve-month calendar, Whitsuntide — generally at the end of

May—can be considered to be on the 'cusp' between the half-way point of the year. The month of May was named after Maia in the Gregorian calendar, based on the Greek myth which spoke of Maia as the mother of Hermes. The Greek word 'maia' means 'mother'. So we can think of May as the month particularly connected with Christ's mother, Mary—the central, 'heart' month in which the Christian festivals have a certain concentration.

According to numerology the number five is the central number, connected with the heart:

    3 6 9 Thinking
    2 5 8 Feeling
    1 4 7 Willing

Spiritual-scientific research undergone by Rudolf Steiner indicates that there are five chambers in the heart. The small yet tremendously vital fifth chamber is the 'space' which is wholly under the domain of Christ. Through this, a Christ-filled heart-force enables us to be empathetic towards our fellow human beings. Mary, the mother of Christ, exemplified the receptive, listening, empathetic quality when Jesus 'poured his heart out' to her in the conversation before the Baptism.[*]

Mother Mary is the archetypal apocalyptic soul of humanity. As a gift from heaven she lived on the earth and her destiny was witnessed by others. Having been born as the hope for the continuation of the Jewish royal line, a child prodigy of high intellect and maturity who was given in service as a 'Temple virgin', she became a refugee and then the mother of seven children, living in a modest community. Her son, also clearly gifted, died young and

---

[*] See *The Fifth Gospel* by Rudolf Steiner.

Mary became a widow twice over. No doubt, after the sorrowful conversation with the other Jesus whom she had adopted, she believed he was going to his death when he left her to be baptised. Jesus never returned home again. And, in a true sense, his ego-being did die, even though he was then active on the earth for a further three years as a completely changed man. This Christ-endowed man even rejected his mother and siblings, as the twelve-year-old Nathan Jesus had once rejected the young mother Mary in the Temple. When he was told that his family were waiting outside for him Christ retorted: 'Who is my mother, and who are my brothers?' (Mark 3:33). Nevertheless, Mary continued to stay close to Christ Jesus and remained his witness to the end. On the one hand, her untold suffering in beholding the execution of Christ cannot be described in words and can probably only be expressed through the visual arts. On the other hand, Mary's insight into the glory of the death on Golgotha and its significance for the earth is illustrated by the tradition that she remained calm and dignified, if grief-stricken. It is said that Mary and the other women followed the procession to Golgotha at a distance and that Mary consecrated each of the places where Christ had stopped on the way.* Thereafter she visited these holy places regularly, living through Christ's path of suffering again and again. Her life became one of total devotion and contemplation until she attained enlightenment and, at her death, her body became light-filled. The disciples saw, clairvoyantly, Mary's soul ascend and rise through all the angelic hierarchies, until she became one with the Christ Being and the all-creator, Father God.

---

*See Anne Catherine Emmerich's commentary on the life of Jesus Christ.

Throughout the centuries since her death, pious people and saint-like women and men have emulated this last phase of Mary's life—living in seclusion, prayer and dedication to the 'Way of the Cross' or in service to others. However, Mary's life as a whole has many characteristics with which modern people can identify; hers was a destiny of hard and bitter challenges. She was, nevertheless, able to attain purification of her soul and her higher self became united with Christ.

In his book *The Childhood of Jesus* Emil Bock says that in Mary, 'The most promising archetype for all human soul efforts had been fulfilled. Human beings were allowed to be witnesses to how the path of the soul, which had led through all moonlike darkness, suffering and trials, ended in the sunlike, radiant elevation.'

When the disciples met for their devotional Pentecost meal, they probably regarded Mary as a mother-figure for their *soul* community of sisters and brothers. After the great Whitsun event, however, she was more aptly the symbol of the *spiritual* community now lead by the Apostles. Today, we can feel united as members of a renewed spiritual community in which the Holy Spirit, as heightened con-sciousness, can enable us to perceive the Second Coming of Christ.

JUNE

The angel said [to Zechariah]: '... your wife Elizabeth will bear you a son, and you shall call him John ... And even from his mother's womb will he be filled with the Holy Spirit ... He will make a well-prepared people ready for the Lord ... I was sent to you to proclaim this message of salvation to you.'

Luke 1: 13–19

And when Elizabeth heard the greeting of Mary, the babe [John] leaped in her womb. And the Holy Spirit filled Elizabeth and she spoke with solemn and mighty words ...

Luke 1: 41–42

And [John] proclaimed ... 'I have baptised you with water, but He will baptise you with the Holy Spirit and with fire.'

Mark 1: 8

Virgin and Child with St Anne and John the Baptist, Leonardo da Vinci

Spiritual Proclamation

The story of the incarnation of the Christ Being on earth begins, according to Luke, with the *proclamation* of an angel, who announced the conception of a child to Elizabeth and Zechariah. That child, the angel communicated, would become the 'herald' of what was about to happen on earth. It would be that child's destiny to help people understand the momentous event for which all religions and cultures, especially the Judaic, had been preparing for ages of time.

In human terms, to proclaim means to make known, sometimes publicly or openly, an important, official or formal message. An angel doesn't 'speak' in the ordinary sense of the word. Rather, a heavenly proclamation resounds in the inner life of the recipient. The recipient may also be an instrument through which the heavenly world 'speaks' to a human audience.

Often, a proclamation is 'called out', with a ritualistic, ceremonial opening and closing and a certain rhythmical or repetitious speech pattern. We have three examples in the Gospels of the heavenly world (the Holy Spirit) speaking through the parents of those children with special destinies, John and Jesus.

In the first example, Elizabeth solemnly declares that Mary is blessed because she will be the mother of the Lord. This proclamation is taken up by Mary in a profound prayer which acknowledges the blessing bestowed upon her and gives praise to God:

> And the Holy Spirit filled Elizabeth and she spoke with solemn and mighty words:

'Blessed are you among all women, blessed is the fruit
  of your body.
How is it that I am so highly honoured that the mother
  of my Lord should come to me?
For see, when my ear heard the sound of your
  greeting, the babe leaped for joy in my womb.
Blessed is she who has trust that the divine promise
  spoken to her will be fulfilled.'

And Mary said:
'My soul grows great in praising you, O Lord of life . . .
See, all future generations will call me blessed.
His power is great, He has made me great, holy is His
  name.'

Luke 1: 42-55

The second example follows soon, with Zechariah's pro-
phetic declaration that his son will be called 'the Herald of
God' and will bring knowledge of the 'new dawn' which
God is about to bestow:

And his father, Zechariah began to speak propheti-
cally, filled with the Holy Spirit:
'All praise be to God, the guiding lord of His people,
  Israel . . .
The meaning of the holy covenant with God is
  renewed in spirit . . .
You, child, will be called the herald of God Most High.
You go before His countenance to prepare the way for
  Him.'

Luke 1: 67–79

John the Baptist's childhood was made easier for him
because his parents fully acknowledged him, so that he

was able to develop freely and find the right conditions in which to prepare for his life's task. The fact that he later left his parents and lived in the loneliness of the desert as a hermit was a sacrifice Elizabeth and Zechariah made for this individuality, who had special, prophetic powers.

The Baptist's moralistic and admonishing teachings were not always received kindly. To say publicly that: 'One is coming ... who will baptise you with the Holy Spirit' was dangerous and subject to jealousy from high quarters. On a deeper level, the understanding of spiritual truths which John was trying to bring about was met by an opposing occult force. Because of the retrograde forces against world development, which human beings continually need to overcome, proclamations and teachings about spiritual truths have always been fraught with danger. For this reason, those in past times who were 'filled with the Holy Spirit' and were moved to speak, did so in rather obscure, metaphorical or symbolic language. Christ himself began speaking publicly in this vein, like John, urging people to 'change their hearts and minds'. He then spoke in parables, before he was able to speak openly to his closest disciples about His Being, His mission, His pre-destined death and His power to overcome death.

Some disciples found it difficult to accept what Christ proclaimed to them. Similarly, after the women had seen the Resurrected Christ, the Apostles did not accept their account. For at least one disciple, the appearance of the resurrected body of Christ was too incredible; only physical substantiality was sufficiently convincing. The gift of tangible proof was given by Christ to Thomas, so that Thomas could understand clearly what the angel had announced to Mary about Elizabeth's conception, namely, that 'in God all things are possible'.

Often, the authoritative nature of a 'spiritual proclamation' makes it difficult to communicate to others; particularly if it states that an event will happen or that a person should change, follow, or simply accept a fact. Usually the Holy Spirit demands an acceptance of something unexpected, strange or seemingly impossible.

Mary's experience of this is one such example — how was she to understand the angel's greeting to her as 'O blessed one' or that she would bear a son, when she had not 'known a man'? She accepted the angel's announcement as a willing servant of the Spirit but found it difficult to communicate this until, finally, the community of disciples was forged at Whitsun. Then, many were filled with the Holy Spirit and were able to talk to others to bring about mutual understanding.

In our own time, information about any subject can be quickly communicated and assimilated. We can understand the geographical, social, economic and political environment of people all around the globe. We can obtain proof of how the physical, natural and cosmic worlds are constructed. We are also coming to understand the human soul through the study of the brain and psychology, through media which focuses on relationships, and through the teaching of emotional language, anger-management and education about different viewpoints. In the present and future we will also need to be knowledgeable about the world of spirit, the Holy Spirit, the Spirit of Christ and the spiritual components of humanity.

We are no longer, as was John the Baptist, preparing for the physical incarnation of the Christ but for His next manifestation as a spiritual, Life-Being. For He promised to come again and we can have faith that He will fulfil His promise. Christ lives now in the invisible aura of the earth—however, it requires our objective understanding of this for Him to become manifest to us, so that we may 'see' His coming-to-earth for the second time.

A prerequisite for developing spiritual knowledge is a feeling of reverence, and celebrating festivals is a means of helping us to develop this sense of devotion. In the month of June, during which the birthday of St John the Baptist falls, we can think of his advice to change our hearts and minds. By burning away what is old we can make way for something new. Perhaps that is why the custom of singing round a bonfire has been adopted at the festival of John as part of a celebration for all ages, in joyful anticipation of a new Christian year.

It is helpful to realize that there are four men named 'John' mentioned in the Gospels, who can be distinguished by their different mothers. Elizabeth was the mother of John, the prophet/Baptist who was later executed. Another disciple, John, brother of James, was a fisherman who followed Jesus and later went out as an apostle together with his brother—his mother, Mary, is mentioned as going to Christ's grave with Mary Magdalene, after the Sabbath following Christ's burial. In Acts:12, Peter is described as standing outside the house of another Mary, the mother of 'John whose other name was Mark'.

Then there was Lazarus, whose mother is not mentioned but who had two sisters, Martha and Mary. This individuality was raised from the dead by Jesus Christ and thereafter known as Lazarus-John, the 'disciple whom Jesus loved'. He who stood at the foot of the cross on Golgotha and of whom Jesus said to his own mother 'See, that is your son', is described by Rudolf Steiner as being 'over-lightened' by the spirit of Elijah, which had previously inhabited the aura of John the Baptist. This was a special process which eventually lead to John the Divine becoming the author of the Gospel of John and the Revelation to John.

After Christ died, John protected and became a spiritual collaborator with Mary. However, the time came when Mary was yet again forced to flee her home country for fear of reprisals. Nevertheless, she remained the mother figure for all the apostles and was the embodiment of the most important proclamation ever given to mankind by the Holy Spirit: the announcement that God would enter the earthly world and lead it towards a new future.

JULY

At Joppa lived a disciple called Tabitha, which translated means Gazelle. She never tired of doing good works and helping deeds of love. In those days she became ill and died. They washed her and laid her out in the upper room, the room of the meal. Since Lydda is near Joppa, and the disciples heard that Peter was there, they sent two men to him and asked him, 'Come to us without delay!' And Peter rose and went with them. When he arrived, they led him to the upper room. There all the women crowded round him, weeping and showing him the clothes and garments which Tabitha had made while she was still living. Then Peter showed them all out, knelt down and prayed; then he turned to the body and said, 'Tabitha, arise!' And she opened her eyes, and when she saw Peter she sat up. He gave her his hand and let her stand up. Then he called the brothers and the women in and led her to them, alive. This became known throughout Joppa, and many felt united with Christ through the faith.

Acts 9: 36–42

The Coronation of the Virgin, Paolo Veneziano

Consciousness For Our Time

We hear of the women followers of Christ and his mother Mary for the last time in the Gospels, when it is described in Acts how they were present in the house where the Whitsun event occurred.

As we progress to the next month in the calendar, so we can progress to the next phase of Christ's manifestation after the Whitsun event. It is recorded repeatedly in Acts that Christ appeared in visions or 'spoke' to the disciples, or that they were filled with the Holy Spirit, which enabled them to communicate assuredly about the spiritual world. The apostles were able to heal in Christ's name and even bring the dead back to life, as Peter did with Tabitha.

Then an extraordinary event happened: the persecutor of the early Christians, Saul, was surrounded by a 'heavenly light' and he heard the voice of Jesus (as did the men who were travelling with him). Saul was blinded for three days until the disciple Ananias healed him with the words: 'May the Holy Spirit fill you.' After that, Saul/Paul developed the 'power of the word' and was able to demonstrate that Jesus was the Christ. He taught and prophesied to many people of all nationalities on his extensive journeys, throughout the rest of his life. Paul also baptised many people into the new Christian faith and twelve of these, in Ephesus, experienced the Holy Spirit fill them and they too 'spoke with tongues of the Spirit and prophesied'.

Paul emphasised the difference between the gift of 'speaking in tongues' (being a channel for spiritual com-munication) and the 'gift of prophesy', which was the ability to interpret spiritual communication so that others could understand and act upon it. It was most important for congregations to teach and learn from one another about Christ in a clear, understandable way. In Acts, it is quoted that both men and women were baptised, converting to faith in Christ and becoming members of various congregations.

Advice was given by Paul about the fidelity of marriage and also of the virtue of being at peace as a single person, male or female. His fellow worker, Timothy, taught that women should be 'adorned with a garment of inner beauty; with devout reticence and inner calm'. He suggested that women should take guidance from men and, rather than be spiritual teachers themselves, should be an example to others through silence and harmonious behaviour.

In the face of this, with our modern consciousness, the month of July is perhaps a time when we can be inspired by many great women who, through the centuries, gave their time, love, artistic talents, intellect, physical strength and lives to the service of the Father, Son and Holy Spirit. When the Movement of Religious Renewal, known as The Christian Community, was formed by priests with Rudolf Steiner in the early twentieth century, the ordination of women priests was accepted in recognition of the ego-development of modern human beings, regardless of gender.

After the conversion of Paul, many other spiritual conversions occurred in individuals throughout the centuries. They also happen in our own time. Such conversions may be experienced by the most unlikely people, who perhaps have no spiritual or religious convictions at all. These events sometimes come as part of a tremendous personal crisis, such as a near-death experience, or during a prolonged, traumatic period. There are many narratives about life-changing conversions to Christianity, as people who undergo the experience of perceiving Christ often feel motivated to talk or write about it.

However, while the impact of such experiences on individuals is tremendous and their stories may be encouraging to those who listen or read about them with an open mind, the modern world remains largely unresponsive towards such accounts. A wall of cynicism exists, even against an objective, logical approach to the existence of the spirit. Conversely, many people seek some form of spirituality as an antidote to the stresses and inhumanity of a highly technical, materialistic culture and find it in non-Christian systems of belief. We live in a particularly barren time where the understanding of the living Christ is concerned, unless we are prepared to consciously work towards it.

July, the seventh calendar month, may remind us of the seven 'I am' sayings, which point us towards the seven-foldness of the Ego-Being of the Christ. While we are striving in our time to be united with the life-forces of the Being of Christ, in future we will develop sufficiently to enable us to become bearers, to some degree, of His ego. With the help of seven candles, we can meditate on these sayings:

1. I am the Bread of Life
2. I am the Light of the World
3. I am the Door
4. I am the Good Shepherd
5. I am the Resurrection and the Life (proclaimed by Christ to Martha)[*]

---

[*] See John 11:25.

6. I am the Way, the Truth and the Life
7. I am the True Vine.

Human beings are seven-fold entities with a physical body, life body, astral body, ego and the possibility of three more highly-developed members: the transformed astral body, transformed life body and transformed physical body.[*] July is an appropriate month for reflecting on the stages of development which the human being has completed, with the help of higher beings, over aeons of time, and the stages which we will develop in the future through our own discipline, inner effort and cooperation with the Christ Being.

The month of July (named after Julius Caesar) is a month concerned with politics, economics and the pleasure of the senses. Many countries in the world celebrate their Independence Day in July for example, and millions of people travel across the globe, spending much money in the leisure sector. It is the time of year when we most 'render unto Caesar what belongs to Caesar' and the earth is bereft of our spiritual consciousness. Therefore it is all the more important that we work inwardly to find some inspiration which forms a connection between the spiritual world and earthly life.

In our time women often have to juggle a career path or job with pregnancy and raising a family, so that they understandably find it almost impossible to create time for contemplation, study or spiritual striving. However, seemingly mundane and practical activities can also be carried out with full consciousness of our true human development and of the evolving world. For example, with young children we can make use of the different rainbow

---

[*] See *Occult Science* by Rudolf Steiner.

colours connected with each of the seven weekdays (see below), eat grains which have a connection with each of the planets, or carry out activities relevant to the forces which each of the seven cosmic spheres gives to human beings on earth:

> Monday — washing/water-painting — rice — purple (Moon: Reflection)
>
> Tuesday — oven-baking (especially bread) — oats — red (Mars: Courage)
>
> Wednesday — eurythmy, nature-walk/gardening — millet — yellow (Mercury: Healing)
>
> Thursday — study day — rye — orange (Jupiter: Wisdom)
>
> Friday — arts and crafts — barley — green (Venus: Beauty)
>
> Saturday — flowers, remembrance verse — corn — indigo (Saturn: Memory)
>
> Sunday — Offering, community/family meal, music — wheat — white (Sun: Christ's community).

As adults we think consciously of the seven cosmic spheres of existence which we inhabited before birth and after death.[*] Indications of these can be shared with older children throughout the weekly rhythm of seven days, perhaps through verses or special tasks. We consider:

> The global community on earth which we are conscious of on Sunday.
>
> The reflective, moon-like element of our thinking needs to be warmed with love on Monday.
>
> The strength and will-forces, to which Mars subjects the earth, can be utilised positively on Tuesday.

---

[*] See *Occult Science*, ibid.

> The healing power of the Christ through the forces of Mercury on Wednesday.
>
> The wisdom and spiritual consciousness of Jupiter which we develop through study, for example, on Thursday.
>
> The beauty and sacrifice of the arts in the service of the spirit, influenced by Venus, on Friday.
>
> Our remembrance of our spiritual past, going back as far as our development on Old Saturn[*], and the 'sheltering power' of those who have crossed the threshold, on Saturday.

July can be the month when we celebrate, in particular, the completion of the seven-year developmental phases of those within a family or community. Thus, every 7, 14, 21, 28, 35, 42, 49, 56 and 63-year-old reaches a zenith of human development[†]. This is an achievement brought about with the help of planetary influences, our guardian angels and other higher beings — so we have much to be thankful for at these important moments in our lives.

While each family or community may have traditional ways of celebrating, any festival should be a new act of creation by the individuals concerned. Within a familiar structure, a creative space should always be given to inspiration from the spiritual world. It is a special privilege to re-enliven the cultural/spiritual life in our modern society — a task with which women, particularly, can identify.

---

[*] See *Occult Science* by Rudolf Steiner.
[†] See *Phases* by Bernard Lievegoed.

AUGUST

Then he turned towards the woman and said to Simon, 'Look at this woman. I came to your house, and you did not wash my feet; but she has wet my feet with her tears and wiped them with her hair. You gave me no kiss; but all the time she has been in the house she has not ceased kissing my feet. You did not anoint my head with oil; but she has anointed my feet with precious ointment. And therefore I say to you: Her many sins are forgiven her, for she has shown much love. But he who is forgiven little also loves little.' And he said unto her, 'You are released from your sins!' The other guests began to say to themselves, 'Who is this, who even forgives sins?' And he said to the woman, 'The power of your trust has helped you. Go in peace!'

And in the time after this he went through the towns and villages, preaching and proclaiming the message of the spirit from the Kingdom of God. The twelve were with him, as well as some women whom he had healed of evil spirits and diseases: Mary from Magdala whom he had freed from seven demons, Joanna, the wife of Chuza, a steward in Herod's service, Susanna and many others.

Luke 7: 44–50, 8: 1–3

Christ and the Samaritan Woman at the Well, Kaufmann

Christ's Healing of Women

Many people spend some time in August recovering from work schedules, the stresses and strains of the fast pace of modern life and the limited access to sunlight, fresh air and nature. A reconnection with unfettered time, space and the elements of fire (sunshine), water, air and earth is essential. It helps restore balance and harmony to the human soul, strengthens the life-forces and brings about healing.

The women in the Gospels (apart from Mary, mother of Jesus and Elizabeth, mother of John) are mentioned, not as disciples but as those who received healing from Christ. As a group, rather than as individuals, these women may be considered to represent the human soul in its many varied aspects. Through His acts the Christ Being planted the seed of healing for all human souls—but there was a special reason why He healed these women. The Holy Spirit (or Healing Spirit) was able to unite with the female soul and could therefore work with the Son to heal humanity. Christ recognized the huge implication of this when, at the marriage celebration in Cana, he asked his Mother the question: 'Woman, what have I to do with thee?' (O Holy Spirit, manifesting in womankind, how can we work together so that your healing force may work through me for the benefit of all human beings?)

The Gospels state that Mary, the holy mother, conceived the being of Jesus spiritually before he was physically born. At the marriage of Cana she officiated the ceremony as a special representative of the indwelling Holy Spirit, a fact which was acknowledged by Christ Jesus. This was his first act as the incarnated Christ Being. We cannot underestimate the importance of his deed, working with the Holy Spirit to change the life-substance of the earth into a new, enlivened substance — symbolized by the change of old wine into best, new wine.

The Gospels relate how, after this, Christ repeatedly balanced the soul state of different women, transforming those who were possessed, sinners, unclean or desperate, into human beings with a new outlook. To women who had, to all intents and purposes, lost their pure connection with the spiritual world, he restored their purity. He realigned these women with their relationship to their Highest Feminine Soul, so that they could fulfil their true destinies as women with tasks on earth — the special destiny of women has always been to conceive the intentions of the spiritual world that influence the cultural and spiritual life of humanity.

Christ's healing of women is related in the following Gospel passages:

> Matthew 8:14, Luke 4:38, Mark 1:29 — healing the fever of Peter's mother-in-law.
> Luke 7:11 — the mother of the young man of Nain.
> Luke 7:36, 8:1 — anointing of Jesus in the Pharisee's house, and the women followers.
> Matthew 9:18, Luke 8:40, Mark 5:21 — woman with the haemorrhage and raising Jairus' daughter.
> Matthew 15:21, Mark 7.24 — healing the daughter of the woman from the region of Tyre.
> John 4:1 — conversation with the Samaritan woman.
> John 8:1 — the adulteress.
> Luke 10:38 — Mary and Martha.
> Luke 13:10 — healing of the woman bent over.
> Mark 12:35, Luke 21:1 — the widow's offering.

Matthew 26:3, Mark 14:1, John 12:1 — anointing in
  Bethany.
John 19:25 — Jesus' mother at the foot of the cross.
Mark 16:9, John 20:11 — appearance before Mary of
  Magdala.

All the passages relate how Christ restored these women's
dignity, hope and faith.

We read briefly how He healed the fever of Peter's
mother-in-law, and we must assume this was the healing
of a physical illness. At first we might think that the healing
of the woman with the prolonged haemorrhage was also
purely a physical matter. Yet the fact that she was ritually
unclean according to the Jewish law and therefore shunned
by society, was for this woman by far the greater burden.
The emotional relief, as well as the deeper, karmic re-
balance between her and the twelve-year old girl, restored
a wholeness to both the souls of these individuals. True
healing comes about when both the karma between one
individual and another and the karma of an individual
within the society of a specific place and time are recognized and lovingly accepted.

Similarly the woman who was not able to straighten her
back could be considered to have been suffering from a
physical condition. However, Christ said she had been
'held bound by the dark might of the enemy for eighteen
years' and declared that she should be released from her
bondage.

He chastised those who criticised him for healing this
woman on the Sabbath, because she was one of their own
kin, a 'daughter of Abraham', whom they treated worse
than an animal. She was misshapen and for her this was
psychologically like being trapped in a cage or tied to a

stake. In giving back her 'uprightness', Christ gave her a dignified place in society and demonstrated the correct attitude we should have towards human beings who suffer from deformity. Such a holy deed was appropriately performed on the holy Sabbath.

Christ restored life itself to the daughter of Jairus, to the son of the widow of Nain and to Lazarus, the brother of Martha and Mary, thereby healing the anguish of grief and familial loss to the souls of these mothers and sisters. He demonstrated great compassion for the depth of soul connection between family members. At the same time He showed how human beings can create new family connections between people unrelated by blood when, with his dying words, he declared that his mother Mary had a new son, John. Christ gave us hope that even beyond the threshold of death a soul–spiritual relationship is possible, as he made clear when he appeared to Mary Magdalene. We further read that his mother Mary was present at the Whitsun event, when a new community was formed. This was between those who were not related but were connected by the indwelling of the Holy Spirit.

Christ did not condemn the 'woman caught in adultery' but rather recognized that men in her presence were captivated by her beauty and were therefore also sinners in their imagination, if not in action. By drawing in the earth, Christ remembered the original separation that came about between male and female sexuality: 'the Lord God made man of dust from the ground ... and woman was made one flesh with man'. This 'adulteress' was both a perpetrator and victim of the attraction between the sexes. Christ therefore released her from the punishment of an unjust law while at the same time exhorting her to 'sin no more'. Through this balanced sentencing, Christ cancelled out the antagonism towards the female sex that was apparent among the male 'law keepers'.

Mention is made several times in the Gospels that women who were possessed by 'unclean spirits' or 'demons' were freed or 'released from their sins' by Christ. This is healing of the psyche. In particular we can follow the complete transformation of the personality of Mary Magdalene, whom Luke says Christ freed of seven demons. About this Mary, the sister of Martha, Christ said she had chosen 'the one thing that shall not be taken away from her'. Mary had attained the state of mind which enabled her to let go of the fear that she would be left destitute if she did not serve the men-folk of her society. At that time women were totally dependent on men to sustain them, and could be assured of survival if they served men who had money, power or religious status. Martha had been conditioned to believe that if she served Jesus and the disciples with ardour, she would be assured practical and spiritual inclusion. But Mary had learned that trust, faith and devotion to the Son, who had been sent by the Father to redeem the sins of earthly life, were the only certain things to ensure the continuation and salvation of the human soul.

Characteristically, Mary Magdalene gave her soul completely to her one, great love. Christ pointed out to the disciples the poor widow who put all she had into the offering box. By this He demonstrated that the true, pure soul of womanhood, capable of giving everything to spiritual devotion, is a noble example to all.

It was to a woman, unhappy in marriage and not of the Jewish race, that Christ first openly said 'I am He [Messiah], speaking to you'. This was a woman who had tried several times to fulfil a happy marriage and, despite repeated disappointment, was still trying. This epitomized her unwavering hope and faith. She was a Samaritan, with whom the Jews avoided contact because the Samaritans worshipped 'without consciousness'. She told Jesus that she had complete trust that the Messiah would come and that He would bring consciousness to her people. Her unfaltering faith was rewarded through her conversation with Jesus when she realized, because he was able to empathize with her soul state, that he was, in fact, the Messiah. The Samaritans had remained true to their faith in the coming of the Messiah, which had been sown like a seed in their souls. Their souls were now like a ripe harvest, ready to be reaped. Because of the Samaritan woman's absolute conviction, her folk were easily persuaded to receive Jesus into their community as the Christ, and to proclaim His salvation to all the world.

Christ Jesus also spoke to the Samaritan woman about the Water of Life: 'Whoever drinks of the water that I give him, his thirst shall be quenched for this aeon of time. The water that I give him will become in him a spring of the water flowing into true life.' The month of August, when people are thirsty for a renewed feeling of well-being, can be experienced as the month when we celebrate the 'water of life' which flows inherently through the Word. The contemplation, study or discussion of the Gospels and other spiritual literature can give us spiritual nourishment for the whole year!

SEPTEMBER

Stand fast, girded about the loins with truth.
Put on the breastplate of the higher life which fulfils our human
  destiny.
Shoe your feet with preparedness to spread the message of peace
  that comes from the angels.
In all your deeds continually hold on to your hearts' vision of
  Christ's presence,
with which you can quench all the flaming darts of the evil one.
Take into your thoughts the certainty of the coming
  world-healing,
that it protect you as with a helmet,
and grasp the sword of the Spirit
which is the word of God which you utter.

Ephesians 6: 14–17

St Michael, Luca Giordano

Balancing Empathy and Logic

The figure of the Angel Michael has always been portrayed as the archetypal hero. He is often on horseback, with helmet, armour and sword, fighting a dragon. Yet, in many paintings his facial features and physique show compassion, grace and agility. He is composed, rather than violent, and the direct gaze and expression in his eyes can be read as his ability to use his intelligence wisely. The best portraiture depicts a wonderful balance of feminine and masculine qualities.

In the apocalyptic times, which have now begun and which will continue into the future, the trials and tribulations which men and women undergo can serve to strengthen both receptivity and independence. Women and men will equally face adversity in future incarnations as balanced, courageous, spiritually aware human beings, becoming members of Christ's community and working actively for the continuing development of humanity and the earth.

Modern scientific development demonstrates that human beings have the intellect to gain knowledge of many detailed aspects of the physical world and the universe. We use the earth's resources to produce manifold goods and can manipulate matter with startling results — sometimes with tremendous benefits, for example, in the field of medicine. Mass-media and instant communication have also made us very aware that we are members of an international humanity. However, we know that the earth's abundance is not finite. This means that we must use our abilities responsibly, for the good of all human beings, trying to improve the life of those who barely survive, and into enhancing the beneficent components of the earth and the universe. Images of Michael depict the courage and steadfastness which are needed to succeed in these tasks.

Nevertheless, a deeper inner strength is required to face the advancing decline of life on earth, which will lead inevitably to the end of the world order as we know it. This strength can only come from the knowledge that the Christ Being is the instigator of new life which will rise out of the ashes of a dead world and with whom we, as human beings, must cooperate in the depths of our souls. The Archangel Michael is our leader in the spiritual hierarchy, who demonstrates the earnestness, solemnity and constancy required by human beings to ensure their own future.

Michael urges us to work with goodwill towards the forming of a global community. Culturally, women have been portrayed over centuries as being the 'weaker sex' — perhaps as a consequence of the general prevailing 'masculine consciousness' which has been necessary to develop our intellectual, analytical and separating forces. This has been a decisive factor in helping human beings eventually to reach a clear understanding of the spiritual world. Nevertheless, women were not always considered to be weaker than men — in older matriarchal societies the women were leaders and were admired for having strong characteristics. Indeed, it is perhaps easier for women to envisage a common community of all women around the world who have empathy for one another, regardless of geographical or political boundaries. After all, many women share the great task of bringing life into the world and of sustaining it, either the life of their own children or of the children borne by other women. War goes against the nature of women and this, therefore, gives a strong foundation for consciously working towards peace, healing and the forging of healthy relationships between all people.

In our modern times, both men and women require strong soul-forces to counteract the inhumanity that threatens society. Materialism will have a degenerating effect on the thinking, feeling and will-forces of human beings, unless people exercise the strengthening of all these three aspects. We can find inspiration in the courage and determination of those who overcome obstacles, for example the many unsung heroes who get up each day in the face of adversity such as disability, bereavement, unfair imprisonment or terminal illness. Can we also find a 'hero' in ourselves which can face the dragon-like anxieties which threaten to pull us down, or help others to do the same? We may think globally of those afflicted by war, disease, famine, poverty or ignorance, and the small ways in which we can help. But there are also ways of reaching out towards people who may be in difficulty, closer to home, in whom we can show a genuine interest.

In late September, when the battle between the warm light of summer and the encroaching cold of winter is being fought, the mornings become grey and foggy, the sun sets earlier and days become noticeably shorter. How can we find the courage not to succumb to apathy, loneliness or befuddled thinking as the world gradually grows darker and humanity is no longer able to draw its strength from nature? When, eventually, materialism can no longer fulfil the needs of the human soul, people will be thrown back on their own 'inner light' to sustain themselves. Like Mary, who conceived Jesus as the vehicle for the Light of the World, we need to conceive the Christ within us. The image of The Woman with the Child (in the Revelation to John) is a picture of our spiritual nature, which is in its infancy and needs to develop fully. This development, however, requires our own conscious effort which Michael inspires us to undertake.

For young people, the academic year starts in the season of Michaelmas, when it is time to struggle back into a work ethic, learn new things and meet social challenges. Whatever our age, September brings a sense of excitement, tinged with apprehension. Our play and relaxation must give way to a greater concentration on work to be done, matters to be tackled, challenges to be undertaken. For all of us, Michaelmas is the time to muster our will-power in order to face the schedules ahead.

In the northern hemisphere we realize now that there is no going back to the summer — the days become cooler, the leaves seem to have imperceptibly turned golden. We want to observe closely, so as not to miss the appearance of orange, russet and brown hues, of dark elderberries and red hips. There are still times in the day when the bright, autumn sun-rays shoot between the branches and foliage. Their straight beams remind us that we should focus our minds with purpose and clarity, like the light-sword wielded in images of Michael.

At this time of year children love to hear stories of heroes and never tire of the idea of adversity, sometimes in the image of a dragon, which is overcome by the human spirit. Older children can study biographies which illustrate some of the draconian, inhuman, retarding forces in the world and how these can be overcome by the heroic attitudes and actions of ordinary people. For adults, September is the month when nature dictates that we make an inner journey, on a path which can lead us towards acknowledgement that there is more to life than that which we see in the material world. If we listen inwardly we may hear a solemn tone—even as outwardly the school bells ring to call young people back to work—a 'Michaelic call', urging our present generation to work towards a positive future.

OCTOBER

Now a great sign appeared in heaven: a woman clothed with the sun, with the moon under her feet, and on her head a garland of twelve stars . . . And the dragon stood before the woman who was ready to give birth, to devour her child as soon as it was born.

Revelation 12:1

Virgin of the Immaculate Conception, Velazquez

The World Soul Working in Daily Life

One interpretation of the picture of the 'woman in heaven' is that it is the image of the pure being who incarnated as the young Mary, who would bear Jesus, the vessel for the incarnation of Christ. We see her before the birth of Jesus occurs. The Imagination shows us that a cosmic plan has been laid and the antichrist forces, in the image of the dragon, are already preparing to oppose Christ on earth.

The vision is not merely a sign, but a 'great' sign. So we may deduce from this that it is also an archetypal image, where the woman represents the soul-archetype of all human beings. In this picture, warmth and light surround the woman. She is within a golden sphere of love, as constant as the ever-rising sun. Her feet stand on the moon, grounded in the rhythmical ebb-and-flow with which the moon influences all life on earth. In the aura around her head, in the thoughts which inspire her, this woman is at one with the cosmos. Interpreting this, we could say that the archetypal human soul exists in three spheres—one which is grounded in the creation of the Father, one which is protected by the love of the sun-being, Christ, and one which is enlightened by the Holy Spirit.

The picture is transformed, after the birth of Jesus, in the painting of Raphael's *Sistine Madonna*. In this image Mary now has the child in her arms. The incarnation and life of Christ will proceed. There is a faint glow of sunlight behind and around Mary's figure—the warmth is transmitted into the more earthly cloak which she wears. Her gaze, unlike in many other religious paintings of the subject, is not directed towards the baby in her arms but outwards towards the universe and the starry worlds, connecting with the higher Being of Christ. Beneath her feet the cold moon with its hardened nature forces has given way to the gentle airiness of clouds. Her tread is light and effortless. In fact, she is no longer on the earth but her consciousness is in the spiritual worlds.

Women, particularly, can be inspired by these archetypal pictures in their daily lives:

'The moon beneath her feet…'

We can be grateful for the rhythm which underlies our bodily existence, influenced by the monthly phases of the moon. This provides a wonderful template which we can bring up from our unconscious, instinctive self into conscious awareness — an awareness that a rhythmical life can bring health, not only to ourselves but to our families and others. This in itself is a huge challenge in the midst of an arhythmical, modern life. The 'dragon' gains ground by causing ill-health and disharmony, which is often brought about by a disorganized, chaotic lifestyle. Waking, sleeping, mealtimes, work, play and quiet times can all be brought into a rhythmical pattern throughout the day. Certain tasks may be delegated to specific days of the week. The months bring different qualities and seasons to enjoy, with activities suitable for the weather, for example. Throughout the year the Christian festivals are great landmarks to celebrate. Their regularity gives us a sense of security and we can celebrate them in traditional and in new, creative ways.

'Clothed with the sun...'

Around a rhythmical structure (rather like the metric foundation of a poem) we need to weave creativity. Creativity brings new life into our existence, just as sunlight causes all things to thrive. It requires imagination to find creative ways of meeting even the most difficult situations. Children certainly provide a wonderful challenge, demanding that adults maintain a correct balance between rhythmic structure and creativity. But this is much easier if children are given sufficient space and time to be creative.

As adults too, we need to give ourselves sufficient allowance for creative pursuits—even if we are not artists by profession. We can all enhance our home or work environment, our clothing, the way we make meals, our spoken or written words. The effect of sunlight in the atmosphere creates all the colours of the rainbow—these colours can have a harmonious, healing effect if we surround ourselves with them. The warmth of the sun's rays stimulates the well-being of all living entities—so we too may bring healing, through the physical and soul warmth we create for those in our care.

'A garland of stars around her head...'

Probably most difficult of all, amidst the distractions of family and work life, is the ability to have clear, well-defined thoughts. We regularly need to practise logical thinking as an exercise! Remembering to think before we act or speak, to plan ahead, to organize our routines and to think back over the the day, in logical backward sequence, are all beneficial activities which help us to gain a conscious control over our lives.

Cosmic Thoughts

The awareness that other Beings also work with our destinies and those of people close to us, is an important aspect to keep in mind. For example, we can meditate on the guardian angels of the children in our care, or pray to them for help.

Keeping in touch with the cultural, social, historical and political developments of nations and where, how and why these aspects interact around the world can remind us that higher beings are at work. Characteristics of the various folk-souls inspire us when they demonstrate resilience, endurance, compassion and selflessness.

It is a challenge to keep up with the scientific and technological advances of our time and to follow the reasoning of those who maintain that all the answers to our existence can be found within proven scientific theories. It is vital to maintain an alertness of how this is affecting our modern society, especially if our main focus is on the daily care of very young children. It requires even greater courage to carry a steadfast consciousness that the universe has 'Beingness'. Highly evolved beings have responsibility for all that develops in each aeon of time. More challenging is the fact that we, in our time, have a hand in that responsibility. Will-power is necessary for us to fulfil our global responsibilities; we need the capacity to listen for the great Michaelic tasks set before us and for putting these into some kind of action.

Raphael's Sistine Madonna

This image represents those moments when we are immersed in prayer or meditation and are released from earthly matters and 'brain-bound' thinking. If we merely managed to attain this state of being 'off the ground', as it were, we would be pursuing a selfish exercise. But at the centre of this esoteric representation is the picture of the Christ child, held close to the woman's heart. This surely reminds us that Christ should be at the centre of any inner work that we undertake. The sacrificial demands of being a parent, godparent, grandparent, or of undertaking any altruistic work for others, help us ultimately to allow the Christ Being to work in the world. If we are able to carry this thought in our hearts, we can be at peace even in the face of adversity.

A picture of the *Sistine Madonna* is a healthy reference in an environment where there are young children or expectant mothers. In the background of this painting we can perceive the 'faces' representing the souls waiting to make the transition from the heavenly worlds to earthly incarnation. At the other end of the spectrum, as October draws to an end we can think of those souls who recently left the earth and crossed the threshold into the spiritual sphere nearest to us. They have contributed to the earth's evolution and continue to do so from there. It is also the end of the Christian year, when we look forward to a new cycle of twelve months in which we can engage our will, feelings and consciousness in the act of attaining the renewal of life granted to us by Christ.

NOVEMBER

Mary said to the angel, 'How can this be, since I have never known a man?' The angel said to her, 'The Holy Spirit will come upon you . . . Indeed, Elizabeth your relative has also conceived a son in spite of her age . . .' And it happened, when Elizabeth heard the greeting of Mary, that the babe leaped in her womb; and Elizabeth was filled with the Holy Spirit.

Luke 1: 34–41

Sistine Madonna, Raphael

The Community of Spirit

The Christian year begins by celebrating the moment (which actually occurred nine months before 25 December) when a heavenly being proclaimed to a woman on earth the most significant spiritual message in human history. The woman, Mary, was so profoundly affected by this enlightening experience that her soul became entirely receptive to the will of the spiritual world, and even her physical body was altered. An announcemnt was also made concerning her cousin, Elizabeth.

The subject of the Annunciation, Conception and the 'Virgin Birth' may pose a puzzle to us in our modern age. In the historic sense, and in many cultures still today, a 'virgin' is considered to be a girl who has not yet begun menstruating. At the other polarity, a woman who is 'barren in old age' would generally be recognized in all cultures as one who has ceased to menstruate. It could reasonably be argued that Mary began her first menstrual cycle at the auspicious moment mentioned in the Gospel and that her older cousin, Elizabeth, was able to conceive within the two-year period after the cessation of menstruation. Conception and pregnancy in both instances, while unusual, are within the realms of physical possibility.

Nevertheless, these rare circumstances highlight the two phases when, for all women, there is an independence of the moon-cycle. Subdued moon-forces meant that sun-forces had a greater access to the souls of these two women with whom we are concerned. The women's individual destinies had the upper hand over their group-soul identities and, further more, they were able to unite with higher forces which accompanied the special human beings wishing to be born to them.

Since the event of Christ's incarnation on earth, many women have the capacity of sensing, or communicating with, the individuality of the child they are carrying in the womb. For example, a woman may understand something of the child's character, disposition and karma, or hear the child's name. Mary and Elizabeth were part of a family within the Essene community, which strove to maintain purity in the souls of its members and, supported by the particular phases we have mentioned above, were able to attain an enlightened state. They were able to conceive spiritual thoughts about the characteristics of their children, and hear the names of their unborn babies: Jesus and John.

Above all, they knew that they were being assisted by angelic forces. Not only did they both have this in common, but Elizabeth understood that Mary was carrying the most important individuality of all—that she was 'the mother of the Lord'. How vital must have been that unreserved recognition of another woman to the expectant Mary! Purity of soul on the one hand and maturity of soul on the other, unencumbered by normal physical demands, allowed a more heightened receptivity of spiritual insight—a perception of the Holy Spirit—by both these women.

The listening quality of both women, indeed of all women, especially during pregnancy, is exemplified in Elizabeth. When she heard Mary, Elizabeth recognized the community of spirit between herself, her younger counterpart and the two unborn boys—her own baby 'leaping' in her womb. The moment was so auspicious that it is mentioned in the Gospel as the time when Elizabeth was 'filled with the Holy Spirit'. The first seed of the community of Christians could be said to have been planted in the souls of these two women, Mary and Elizabeth.

Not only did Elizabeth give Mary empathetic support, but this was reciprocated by Mary, who remained with Elizabeth for the last three months of her pregnancy. Once John was born to Elizabeth, her husband Zechariah, relatives and friends took on that supportive role. Then Mary returned to the protection of Joseph, to whom she was betrothed.

In Luke's Gospel it seems that Mary was alone in the knowledge of her destiny for the remainder of her pregnancy, although Joseph travelled with her to Bethlehem for the census. There she gave birth in a lonely place. Some shepherds heard the angelic 'harmony of spheres' and understood the proclamation that the Lord had been born to Mary. However, once they had seen the child they returned home, and nothing is reported of Joseph's reaction to their visit. It was only at the time when his parents took Jesus to the Temple to consecrate him to God, that Mary once again had the opportunity to feel a communion of the Holy Spirit with someone else—the Gospel states that the Holy Spirit was upon Simeon. Simeon was happy to die after he had seen the child Jesus, knowing that God had given humanity 'a light which leads the peoples of the world to revelation'.

Having experienced the visitation of the Angel of the Lord, communed with Elizabeth, the shepherds, Simeon and Anna the prophetess, Mary had further confirmation of the special incarnation of her child when he was twelve-years-old. We are told that she kept Jesus' words

'Do you not know that I must be in my Father's house?' in her heart.

Like Mary, we may be filled with the Holy Spirit, as revelation or inspiration in our hearts. We feel united with one another in this as a community on earth, and also with those souls who have died with whom we have a connection. We can develop a connection, too, with souls who will be born in the near future. If we look carefully at the painting of the *Sistine Madonna* by Raphael, we see the curtain, or veil, drawn back to reveal the cosmic sphere from which all human beings originate and to which we all return.

As we journey on an inner pathway towards Christmas, striving to create quiet moments for contemplation, we find that we are closest at this time of the year to the spiritual arena nearest to earthly life. This is the sphere in which angelic beings, along with human souls connected to the earth in the recent past or the near future, dwell.

We can ponder the fact that human beings who have crossed the threshold into the spiritual world are very active, working to help fellow souls who have died but who may have lost a consciousness of their divine origin. Much work is also required to help souls on earth and also in preparing the state of the earth for future incarnations. The dead are constantly communicating with us through indirect events and signs, which we are beginning to understand more clearly in our time. Christ himself is the most highly evolved angelic being of this sphere, and through Him we remain united with discarnate souls in a community of the heart.

In the month of November we remember those who have sacrificed their lives for an ideal. We can light a candle for them in a special place and engage in meditative prayer for them. Nature may seem to desert us at this time of year—however, one bright light may remind us that Christ's deed of uniting with the earth can give us all eternal hope.

We recall the legend of St Martin, who gave half his cloak one cold, late autumn night to a poor beggar who, unbeknown to him, was Christ in disguise. It reminds us of Christ's saying: 'Whatsoever you do to the least of my brothers, that you also do to me.' There are many inspirational biographies about people who have found themselves in dangerous, hopeless situations, who have been granted a 'light in the darkness' by spiritual grace.

Our small candles on earth are reflected in the myriad of stars in the dark November sky. We watch for shooting or falling stars, remembering women all over the world who fall pregnant, as souls make their way down to earthly incarnation hoping to be with their chosen parents and, ultimately, to becoming free members of a community of spirit on earth.

DECEMBER

And in that neighbourhood there were shepherds in the field. They guarded and protected their flocks through the night. All at once, the angel of the Lord stood before them, and the light of the revelation of God shone about them ... And the shepherds returned home; heavenly light shone forth from the words with which they praised God, the Ground of the World, for all that they had heard and seen.

Luke 2: 8–9, 20

'I AM the good shepherd. The good shepherd lays down his life for his sheep.'

John 10: 11

Jesus says to Simon Peter, 'Feed my lambs' ... and He says to him, 'Be a shepherd to my little sheep' ... And Jesus says to him, 'Feed my sheep.'

John 21: 15–17

St Sebastian and Irene, George de La Tour

Pastoral Work

Nowadays many occupations are carried out during the night-time hours. People who do not work a night-shift might experience what this is like when they become parents. Mothers and fathers can recognize that time in the early hours when a small baby must be tended to—a phenomenon which breaks the normal routine or rhythm and therefore can seem irksome and exhausting. However, a calm, quiet environment, with the use of a candle for light and no daytime sensory input, can make the night vigil a peaceful time to be savoured. In such a moment, the world makes no demands upon us to be active, noisy or productive. Instead, we have the possibility just to 'be'.

Meditative prayer at times when we find ourselves in conducive circumstances, or when we consciously make a time available, can help us to see new ways of approaching world questions. It can assist us to listen and to hear, beyond the silence, the messages which beings in the spiritual world are trying to convey to us. Often these missives only make themselves known if we observe occurrences during the day and learn to read them in a certain way. Such ideas can be tested objectively, even if we have to wait some time for a confirmation of them. Our understanding may be increased in surprising ways, if we are sufficiently humble to allow spiritual beings to 'speak' to us, unhindered by our preconceptions. Christ-centred prayer ensures that we communicate with the spiritual world in our 'seeing' and 'hearing' in a healthy way.

Two thousand years ago there were people awake at night, such as the guards of town-gates and those who watched over animals, or mothers who tended their babies. But the shepherds of the Gospel were in such a quiet, contemplative mood during their night-watch that they were receptive to inspiration from the spiritual world. Other human beings, of whom there is no record, may have been affected like the shepherds — we can wonder who, in that moment of time on earth, was in a similar, open state to receive inspiration from the angelic spheres — even if they were not in the geographic vicinity of Bethlehem. A seer, whoever this was at the time, was able to see the aura around the shepherds when they received their revelation and when they talked about it afterwards. Luke later recorded in his Gospel that 'heavenly light shone forth from their words' — an inspired description of events.

I am the Good Shepherd

People who look after very young children for any length of time experience how children draw on the life-forces of the adults around them. Similarly, all of us, whatever our age, draw on the life-forces of the Christ. This is because our own forces could not of themselves withstand the impact of modern communication-technology, pollution, mass food and drug production, and materialistic thinking. Of course, some people are able to avoid this onslaught, and it certainly behoves parents to take responsibility for protecting their children from it whenever possible. Christ not only gave up his physical body so that he could enter the field of human death, he also infused the earth's life-sphere with renewed strength. It is within this aura that He lives and from where He protects all life on earth as 'The Good Shepherd'.

The Latin word for shepherd is 'pastor' and from this we get the modern term 'pastoral care'. Parents are naturally the pastoral carers of their children and so are their children's teachers. Priests and social workers also have this task in a vocational capacity. Pastoral care is an earthly deed which we can do for one another out of love, understanding, experience or specialist training. We may have compassion for the plight of other human beings, even if we have no personal connection with them, and may decide to help their pastoral needs by donating to a charity, for example. Perhaps we find the subject of welfare issues and pastoral support an interesting one and endeavour to help people through a formal, professional relationship. Or it may be our responsibility to support those who rely on us in our personal lives — we may give pastoral advice out of empathy with those to whom we are close.

However, it is a modern phenomenon that, while there is a growing awareness of the importance of emotions, psychological health, counselling and therapy, there are also issues which seem to continually stretch our ability to help in this way. All reading, case studies, strategy meetings, record-keeping and even religious conviction can be to no avail in certain circumstances. Yet out of crises and disasters, new relationships form between human beings and within communities. Paradoxically, materialism loses its power when people are struck by shock and grief.

But can we only stand by and watch helplessly while humanity suffers these hardest of lessons? What if a catastrophic or deeply hurtful event touches someone close to us and it is outside our ability to help? There are times when we may feel it is impossible to 'feed' or 'be a shepherd to others' in the pastoral sense. Not knowing what to do or say gives us the opportunity to ask the spiritual world for help, through meditative prayer. This is something we can do alone, in a small group of 'two or three met together', or in a community. The more we do this with earnestness, being open to the help that can stream to us from the angelic spheres, the more will human beings develop as co-workers with higher beings in the cosmos. Christ is the great mediator between humanity and the Healing Spirit, which comes to our aid and comforts us in times of need.

We can use the picture of the shepherds watching over their flocks at night as a guide to engendering the appropriate atmosphere which can support us during Advent, Christmas and the Holy Nights. Their sheep had their woollen coats to give them warmth against the harsh elements — we too can create both physical and soul warmth by telling stories or reading by the fireside. The food we prepare can have this element of warmth and nourishment. The way in which we give thanks for our meals also gives us food for the soul.

The shepherds provided protection for their flock. So can we strive to create a safe, secure environment for children and people of all ages in our communities. For this reason the Christmas season, particularly, is an appropriate time to give help providing food, shelter and companionship for people less fortunate than ourselves. The stars in the night sky, especially the star which led the shepherds to the place of Jesus' birth, may remind us to bring light into our lives and the lives of those in our community, whether it be candlelight or learning about the enlightened ideas of human beings who have brought gifts into the world through their thinking.

Just as the shepherds heard the sound of angelic singing

around them in the aura of the earth, so is music a vital artistic gift at this time of year, helping to create a connection between us and the spiritual heights.

Children and adults alike can simulate a journey through Advent time towards the culmination of the midnight hour on Christmas Eve, by walking round a spiral path formed of greenery. This will spiral inwards towards a candle, from which smaller candles are lit and placed along the way by participants, until the darkness of the space shines with ever-growing light.

While the Advent journey gradually lead inwards, the Holy Nights, between 25 December and 6 January, provide a period for consolidating this inwardness. It is a time for quietly contemplating the twelve months ahead, especially focusing on their connection with the planetary spheres in the cosmos and the gifts or challenges which these will bring to humanity through the coming year.

We can feel immense gratitude throughout this special season for the great gift of the Son, who was given to us by the heavenly Father, to lead us into the future. This is the real reason why we give gifts to one another, share food and endeavour to create a supportive, truly pastoral ambience. It inspires us to work throughout the year in a caring way, thus contributing to the development of earth as a planet of love.

Truly, women today can lead the way towards this ideal!

Part Two

TWELVE WOMEN WHO CHANGED THE WORLD

Hrotsvite (Roswitha) of Gandersheim
(*c.* 935–1000)

Over a millennium ago a woman with exceptional ability was fortunate to live in circumstances which were conducive to expressing herself through the written word. She was the first woman playwright and the first writer to transcribe Christian themes into classical verse.

We don't know the exact date of her birth, although Roswitha herself wrote that she was born several years after the death of Otto, father of Henry the Saxon, in 912. She lived in Saxony under the rule of Otto I, Otto II and Otto III. When Otto III died in 1002, the Ottonian rule came to an end. It had been an especially illustrious time for the Saxons, who had won military victories throughout Germany and the surrounding countries, including Italy. The connection between Germany and Italy brought about a tenth century renaissance of art and literature and Otto I was particularly enthusiastic to enrich the cultural life of Saxony. He built a large royal library, which he extended into several abbeys that were under his court rule. Otto had promised to defend the Pope, who crowned him Emperor in 962. Because of the dependency of the papacy on the royal court, Otto ruled many religious institutions and several of his relatives were clerics, who sometimes combined their secular and episcopal positions. His brother, for example, was both a bishop and a duke.

One of the abbeys which was given royal privileges was at Gandersheim. It was run by Gerberga, Otto's niece. Otto gave the abbey complete independence and allowed the abbess to have her own court of law, coinage, army and a seat in the Imperial Diet. Because girls from Saxon nobility were sent to the Gandersheim Abbey, we might assume Roswitha had an aristocratic background, although nothing is known about her childhood.

It is not certain at what age Roswitha entered the abbey but we know that she was a canoness rather than a nun. This meant that she could keep any property she owned, retain servants, have visitors, and remain a member of her family. She made vows of chastity and obedience, but not of poverty. So Roswitha lived in freedom from the rule of Church and State, nevertheless under royal protection, with the benefit of access to an education and sources of literature. She studied the scriptures, lives of the saints, liberal arts and the classical works of Roman writers such as Terence.

Roswitha wrote that she was privileged to have been taught by a kind and wise teacher, Riccardis, among others, and then by Gerberga her abbess, who had herself received an excellent education as a Saxon princess. Roswitha began writing very tentatively and stated that she destroyed all her early attempts. She eventually decided that, with God's help, she should exercise her talent rather than let it lie dormant. She chose to write in classical verse form, which requires a high degree of competency and, rather than confine her subject-matter to the lives of local saints, the scope of her writing encompassed early Christian themes, historical heroes and contemporary European martyrs.

Roswitha wrote eight legends about Christian saints, seven of which were in the classical poetic form of dactylic hexameter. They were poems about Mary the mother of Jesus, Christ's Ascension, Dionysius and Agnes the early

Christian martyrs, and a contemporary tenth-century Spanish martyr, Pelagius. Another is about a French knight from the eighth century, named Gongolf. Two other legends, about the Greek saints Theophilus and Basilius, are of great importance because they are stories of how these men sold their souls to the devil and were saved by God through their repentance—thus giving rise to the theme of Faust in later classical western literature. Roswitha's sources for these works came from the apocryphal gospels, Latin translations of Greek or early Christian narratives and French writings.

She wrote an explanatory note after this collection of work which stated that her sources were from reputable, classical authors—however, she indicated that translations of these may have been inaccurate. She relied more readily on the direct, contemporary source of an eyewitness of the martyrdom of Pelagius, whom she interviewed personally. Clearly, this explanation demonstrates the objectivity and thorough research Roswitha undertook in her work.

A theme occurs in some of Roswitha's writing which emphasizes the salvation of young wayward or older corrupt men, by women. In *Basilius*, for example, a young couple get married despite the fact that the girl has been pledged to a convent. After the marriage, the girl realizes they have sinned and begs forgiveness for her husband, which the bishop Basilius gives in Christ's name. Roswitha points out that although women are 'the weaker gender', they can act as instruments of divine mercy. She is also at pains to point out, in her prologue of *Basilius*, that a female writer such as herself relies on inspiration and assistance from God. She hopes that the reader will therefore praise divine grace, rather than deride the writer because of her innate weaknesses.

After this work Roswitha composed six plays which are considered to be the first Christian dramas. One of these plays portrays a young man who falls in love with a married woman. The woman, although innocent, prays for death rather than ruining the young man's life. After both she and the young man are resurrected by St John, the man — Calimachus — converts to Christianity. The woman — Drusiana — then asks if she may intercede for the life of Calimachus' accomplice and is granted the grace to do so. She thus becomes the instrument of salvation of two men.

In another play the wicked Roman governor, Dulcitius, orders the execution of three young Christian women who have insulted him. Emulating Terence's comedies, Roswitha portrays the governor as a fool who ends up embracing dirty pots and pans rather than the girls whom he desires.

In her play *Sapientia*, the women demonstrate intelligence and wisdom which put the wicked Emperor Hadrian to shame. He tortures the three young daughters of Sapientia (Wisdom) but they are able to bear the pain by remembering their mother's prayers. The mother outwits the emperor by confusing him with a complicated explanation of Boethius' number theory. In the play Sapientia praises God for giving humanity the possibility of understanding science. Indirectly, Roswitha displays her own education and intellectual ability through the words of her characters.

Roswitha does not shy away from licentious themes, as in her plays about prostitutes. In these, although the women are persuaded to atone for their sins by monks, they are able to redeem themselves and eventually earn a place in paradise through the strength of their devotion and asceticism, unlike the men who are tempted by sexual desire.

In explaining why she had chosen such themes, Roswitha stated that she had emulated the work of Terence but contrasted the wicked behaviour of human beings with the forgiveness of Christ. She wrote:

> the more seductive the unlawful flatteries of those
>   who have lost their sense /
> the greater the Heavenly Helper's munificence /
> and the more glorious the victories of triumphant
>   innocence are shown to be /
> especially /
> when female weakness triumphs in conclusion /
> and male strength succumbs in confusion.

She indicates furthermore that, as the tenth century view of women was that they should remain uneducated and weak, so should greater acknowledgement be afforded to the God-given talent which is granted to a female writer by grace. In this she shows humility and perhaps some irony between the lines. The society in which Roswitha lived was strongly patriarchal, and educated women were not allowed to assume that they could teach men. By cleverly using Terence's sense of comedy and dramatic form, Roswitha was able to indirectly teach Christian values and uphold the equality of women. She tried to live up to the meaning of her name, which is 'strong voice'.

Roswitha also wrote two epics and a short poem in Latin verse, as well as several other letters and notes. All her work was kept in the monastery of St Emmeram in Regensburg in the late tenth century, and twelfth and thirteenth-century copies were made. In the sixteenth century interest in Roswitha's work was re-kindled, when these earlier manuscripts were discovered and published. Her work was published in the seventeenth, eighteenth and nineteenth centuries and has since continued to be published in several languages.

In our own century the Roswitha Prize is annually given to female writers in Bad Gandersheim and, at the close of the summer season of the Gandersheimer Domfestspiele, the Roswitha Ring is given to the most outstanding actress every year. Fame was afforded Roswitha on the website of an American feminist drama group in 2006, called the Guerilla Girls on Tour, which challenged any theatre production company to put on a play by Hrosvitha, the first female playwright, rather than a Greek tragedy. The First Annual Hrosvitha Award would be bestowed on the play produced. However, recognition of Roswitha's contribution to drama and to Christian writing remains limited, despite its importance.

Given the privileged and exceptional destiny in which she found herself around a thousand years ago, Roswitha took this as an opportunity to develop her mind and spirit in the service of Christ.

Clare of Assisi
(1194–1253)

The name Chiara, or Clare, means 'clear light'. Clare of Assisi lived up to her name because she developed the capacity of clear, spiritual vision. She was also brave — at a young age she had the courage to turn away from the cultural norm of her day and to defy her father and male relatives, in order to follow a life of complete obedience to Christ. Later in her life, she refused to obey the decree of the pope, who wanted to compromise her ideals.

She was born in 1194 in the Italian town of Assisi to a noble family: her father was the Count of Sasso-Rosso. Both Clare and her mother, Ortolana, were pious and generous to the poor. As was the custom, a marriage was arranged for Clare when she was 15. However, she announced that she wanted to wait until she was older before accepting this path, even though early marriage was traditional for Italian girls at the time.

One day during Lent, Clare heard Friar Francis give a sermon in the church of St George in Assisi. She was so moved by this and the fact that Francis, by all accounts, spoke to her of her calling, that she secretly decided to run away from her family and join him. On Palm Sunday, when she was 18, she and her family attended church, wearing their fine clothes. While the rest of the congregation were being given small crosses made of palm-leaves, Clare seemed to be transported and her face was radiant. As she seemed unable to move, the priest came to her specially to give her the palm-cross.

That night, Clare ran away to Francis' small chapel, where he disguised her in rough friars' garments. She was determined from then on to live in poverty and obedience to the Holy Gospel. As Francis had no nunnery at the time, he took her to a Benedictine convent for safety. When her father eventually heard where she was, he and her uncles made several attempts to bring her back home. However, Clare resisted so vehemently that finally they relented to her chosen way of life. Not long after, Clare's sister, Agnes, joined her. Francis ensconced them, with some other girls who wanted to follow Francis' rule, in a small house next to the Church of St Damiano, on the outskirts of Assisi.

At the age of 22, Clare was made the superior of the house by Francis and he gave her his rules with which to run the convent. These rules insisted on poverty (including no ownership of property by the community), the possession of only one tunic and no shoes. The nuns were only to accept food that they were given by others, to speak little and to lead a life of service to the sick and poor. It was a life of simplicity and austerity in which the nuns slept on the floor and abstained from eating meat. Clare herself ate very little and had to be persuaded to take more nourishment when she became ill. She also extended the ideal of servitude to her own house; looking after the other nuns when they were ill, tending their sore feet, and refusing to accept any recognition for helping others in need.

Clare only took to her bed when she fell ill. When she was unable to attend mass and partake of the sacrament she reported that she could see the whole ritual clairvoyantly on her wall. Because of this, St Clare has since been declared the patron saint of television and telecommunication.

Another time, when she was ill in bed, a group of

Saracens were about to siege the city of Assisi. Clare asked to be taken on her mattress to the city-gates where she partook of the sacrament. This action apparently affected the infidels so much that they turned away. Later, however, one of Emperor Frederick II's generals was successful in taking Assisi hostage for several days. Clare decided that, as the city had supported her convent, she and the nuns should make a concerted effort to help save Assisi. The Poor Clares (as they had become known) prayed day and night in deep earnestness, which seemed to have had some effect, as the siege against Assisi was eventually given up. For this reason, Clare, along with Francis, was later named the patron saint of Assisi.

Several cardinals, bishops and even the pope came to consult Clare during her lifetime. Although she never left the convent of San Damiano, through correspondence Clare was instrumental in founding several convents all across Italy, in France, Germany and Bohemia. Her own mother, aunt and friends eventually joined the Order. The pope decreed that the nuns should have communally-owned property but Clare fought for their right to absolute poverty and never wavered from the original rules of St Francis. On account of this she was often called 'alter Franciscus'. She also resisted the idea of total separation between the nuns and the Franciscan friars, seeking to continue Francis' original ideal of a community of brothers and sisters in complete obedience to the Gospel. Nevertheless, the nuns vowed to spend their lives in 'enclosure', engaged in manual labour and prayer; unlike the friars who led an itinerant lifestyle.

Clare governed as abbess of the Franciscan order of nuns for forty years and was always the first to get up and light the candles and ring the bell for morning prayers. The nuns often observed that her face shone with a radiance after she had been praying.

Although it has never been verified, when Francis visited Clare, two streams of light were reportedly seen crossing the sky above the house where they met. Towards the end of his life, Clare tended Francis during his illnesses until his death. The Passion according to St John was read when Francis died; a scripture which Clare afterwards learned by heart. The same text was read out when Clare herself died, twenty-seven years later.

During her own illness leading to her death, Clare continued to labour, spinning an exceptionally fine thread from which she made over a hundred altar cloths, which she gave to the churches in and around Assisi. She died at the age of 59, just after the papal bull declared that her rule of complete poverty could continue to govern Clare's Order of Poor Ladies. Eventually the order was renamed The Order of St Clare.

The Poor Clare Sisters still have federations today and there are over 20,000 sisters in more than seventy countries throughout the world. However, each monastery of The Order of St Clare is autonomous and unique. The sisters live in joyous poverty, in small family-size groups, serving the local community wherever they are.

After Clare's death, the remains of this exceptionally devoted woman were buried deep beneath the high altar of a completely new basilica built in her honour, where they remained for six hundred years. When these were discovered in the nineteenth century, her skeleton was found to be in perfect condition. It was transferred to the Basilica of Santa Chiara in Assisi, where it can still be seen today, in the shrine built especially for her.

Clare's undaunted spirit of unworldliness brought a

renewal of obedience and discipline to the Church in the late twelfth and early thirteenth centuries, and a deeper sense of morality into West European civilization.

Her courage and inner strength of conviction continue to be shining examples, raying down the centuries into our own time.

Eleanor of Castile
(1241–1290)

Queen-Consort Eleanor and King Edward I of England formed a long-lasting marriage–partnership which enjoyed many adventures and achievements in the face of difficult, often dangerous, times.

Eleanor was a beautiful woman who brought colour and gaiety to the English court. She loved fine things, including tapestries with which she lined her castle walls and coloured glass, which she had commissioned for her windows. Eleanor was educated, intelligent, loyal and utterly devoted to her faith. She showed tremendous fortitude and courage as a woman in the context of medieval life.

She was brought up in Seville in Spain where she lived with her mother, Joanna of Castile, her father, King Ferdinand III and her brother, Alfonso. The household had a literary atmosphere with a large library containing books on every subject, to which (unusually for a girl) the young Leonor of Castile had access. Her father was involved in many military campaigns against the Moorish 'infidels' and, in honour of this, was later named a saint by the Catholic church. He died when Leonor was eleven years old. Her brother, Alfonso, became king and soon began negotiating a political marriage for his sister. At this time, the King of England, Henry III, went to war with Spain in order the keep the last English stronghold at Gascony, France. As part of the peace treaty between the two countries, Henry asked for Leonor to become the wife of his son, Edward. Alfonso agreed to this, with the proviso that the marriage took place five weeks before Michaelmas, which coincided with Edward's knighthood ceremony. In haste, Edward, at the age of 15, sailed to Las Huelgas, where he was knighted by King Alfonso and afterwards married to Leonor, who was then 13-years-old.

It was customary for arranged childhood marriages to be formalized, although these were not necessarily consummated until the children were older. However, it is recorded that, during the year following this marriage, Eleanor (as she was now named) gave birth to a stillborn daughter. This took place in France, on the journey towards her new home in England. So Eleanor had experienced marriage, pregnancy, stillbirth and removal from her home and country, all by the time she was 14. Thereafter, she did not fall pregnant again for nine years, during which time she was educated in the language, ways and customs of her husband.

Perhaps Eleanor and Edward fell in love at first sight, or they grew to love one another, or were bound by their religious vows. Either way, they became almost inseparable and their marriage lasted for thirty-six years. Unusually for a monarch at the time, there is no evidence that Edward had a mistress, nor did he have any children outside his marriage. Edward had a somewhat dour personality and Eleanor seemed to bring out the better side of him. She travelled with him on military and political business in England and Europe and on a crusade to the Holy Lands. Notwithstanding her husband's gruelling schedule and fierce campaigns in England, Wales and Scotland, Eleanor bore him sixteen children.

Eleanor was strong enough to have a child almost every year, whether travelling abroad or at home. However, she also experienced the bitter loss of several of her children, who either died as babies or in childhood. One of these, John, died while in the care of his uncle when Eleanor and Edward were away for nearly four years on a Holy Crusade. During that time, Eleanor gave birth to two daughters in Palestine. Only one of them survived, named Joanna of Acre, after her birthplace. Eleanor's last child, who was to become Edward Prince of Wales, was born in a make-shift tent outside the building-site of Caernarfon Castle.

Eleanor and Edward were second cousins once removed, because Eleanor's great-great-grandmother was Eleanor of Aquitaine, who was queen-consort to Edward's great-grandfather, Henry II. Apart from this filial relationship, they both shared a deep religious faith. One of the aspects of their religious belief was in the Divine Right of Kings and in Edward's special destiny.

Edward had been named by his father, who idolized his saintlike ancestor, Edward the Confessor. Unusually, although Edward was the fourth king to carry the name, he named himself Edward I, which was really the Confessor's title. He also had a keen interest in King Arthur, removing Arthur's bones from Glastonbury and celebrating his conquest of Wales by constructing a simulated 'Round Table' in Nevin, Caernarvonshire. Edward was not averse to creating a kind of empire in Wales, razing the Welsh Conwy Castle to the ground, removing Llewellyn's bones from the site and building a brand new castle. During Edward's construction of another castle at Caernarfon the body of Constantuis, believed to be the father of Constantine, was discovered. This gave rise to the speculation that Constantine himself may have been born on the site, formerly Roman Segontium, which was said to be the stronghold of Magnus Maximus, a usurper emperor.

Edward had the castle designed as a replica of the castle in Constantinople, which he and Eleanor greatly admired. On the way back from the Holy Lands they had been received by the pope and in Tuscany and Lombardy the king had been hailed by the people as 'Emperor Edward'!

Edward undertook Europe's most ambitious medieval building project as part of his campaign to control Wales, overseeing the costly construction of the castles at Rhuddlan, Conwy, Flint, Harlech, Caernarfon and Beaumaris, as well as reconstructing several other Welsh castles. The new castles were served by 'bastide towns' which were built around the castle sites. Edward also built the Tower of London as one of his first projects as king. Eleanor, too, undertook building projects of mansions and gardens, which she loved. She acquired much land, encouraged by Edward and his administrators and for which she received rent, so that she would not need to obtain money from government funds.

Eleanor was the first queen-consort of England to acquire personal financial power and this set a precedent for later queens. She was cultured and well-read, employing scribes to copy books for her. She also had an illuminator, who resided in the royal household, to illustrate them beautifully. She was a patron of literature and commissioned many new books to be written, with subjects ranging from chess to the existence and purpose of angels. She was also the patron of Dominican work and research in the universities of Oxford and Cambridge. Eleanor founded several Dominican priories in England. She had plans to found one near her palace at Langley Regina (now Kings Langley in Hertfordshire) but this was not realized until after her death, when her son, Edward II, built it in his mother's honour.

Eleanor was a devout Catholic and she put her faith into practice, accompanying her husband on the eighth Crusade to the Holy Lands. This entailed travelling across Europe and then sailing by ship—a journey which took well over a year. During their time in the Holy Land an assassination attempt was made on Edward's life and he was wounded by a poisonous dagger. It was said that Eleanor tried to suck out the poison, although this story is not verified. Her husband survived, but it was not the only time that Edward's life was spared. In 1288, in Gascony, Eleanor and Edward were sitting with their backs to a window during a storm when a bolt of lightning passed between them and struck two ladies-in-waiting, who were standing in front of the couple. On another occasion, Edward was playing chess when he suddenly arose and left the game, for no apparent reason. At that moment part of the roof collapsed, killing Edward's opponent.

Eleanor devoted her life to her husband, who was a strong soldier, statesman and a devout Christian. He in turn adored her, for she accompanied and supported him in all his affairs, although she had no official political role. She enjoyed music, dancing and socializing. When Edward refused to attend ceremonies, such as weddings, she arranged that the minstrels went and played for him while he sat alone in the castle. She filled her gardens with orange and lemon trees as well as vines, exotic plants and flowers. Eleanor was sometimes criticized for supporting her relatives but she was careful to arrange marriages for her female cousins to English barons, so that any wealth would remain in England. Certainly, she was known to regularly give alms to the poor.

Queen Eleanor died, at the age of 49, on her way to meet her husband, who was fighting the Scots. He was so devastated by her death that famously he had crosses erected at all the stopping places of her funeral procession, the most well-known remnant being Charing Cross. Although Edward married again several years later, he commemorated Eleanor's death every year for the rest of his life.

Eleanor of Castile was a faithful and supportive wife, mother, patron and queen.

Catherine of Siena
(1347–1380)

Catherine was a child with special abilities. These served her well when she later became a Christian emissary to politicians and church authorities, on whom she had an unusually powerful influence for a woman of her time.

She was born under difficult circumstances, when Italy was suffering from an epidemic of the Black Plague. Her mother had had twenty-two children already when, at the age of 40, she gave birth to twin girls. Unable to care for them both, she gave one of the girls to a wet-nurse to tend. This daughter sadly died. However, Catherine was nursed by her mother and thrived. She was a happy child, whom her family nicknamed 'Euphrosyne', meaning 'joyous'. Although Catherine's sister died, another girl was born to the family who was given the twin's name, Giovanna.

Catherine was only five-years-old when she had a vision of Christ with the apostles, Peter, Paul and John. Already, at the age of seven, she made up her mind to devote her life to Christ. Her parents had other plans, however, and when Catherine's older sister died leaving a widower, they assumed that Catherine would marry the surviving husband. This man, apparently, had not behaved well towards the older sister. Her older sister confided in Catherine that she had refused to eat, in protest against her husband. This was what instilled the idea of not eating in Catherine and was the beginning of her anorexia, which, tragically, lead ultimately to her death.

In order to make herself less attractive Catherine cut her long hair and refused to marry. However, she also rebelled against joining an 'enclosed' convent and decided instead to serve her family. She made a 'cell' in her mind where she could retreat, and pictured her parents as Jesus and Mary and her brothers and sisters as the disciples. She spent her days in prayer and servitude.

When she had a vision of St Dominic, Catherine wanted to join the Order of Dominicans as a tertiary, to which her parents agreed. Catherine continued to live at home in almost total solitude and silence. She did not eat with her family, saying that she would rather be nourished by heavenly grace. Neither did she possess anything, pre-ferring to give away food and clothing to the poor. She learnt to read, from the Dominican nuns, and spent many hours studying.

At the age of 21, Catherine experienced a 'mystical marriage' with Christ, and was given her mission to go out into the world. She worked in hospitals and shelters, helping the poor and sick. Her humble, deeply religious aura caused a number of people to follow and support her. They no doubt afforded Catherine some protection in her travels round the country, when she visited Florence and other cities in northern and central Italy. On these visits she preached a 'total love of God' and urged people to reform and repent, as there was a growing anti-papal movement in Italy at the time.

In Pisa she openly opposed those who were against the pope, and gave her support to some devout people who wanted to go on a new Holy Crusade. Another event occurred in Pisa, which Catherine did not make public: she received the stigmata.

Although she could read, Catherine was not yet able to

write and needed scribes to help her. She dictated letters, not only to her followers, but also to those who had political authority. She wanted to help bring about peace between the Republics and Principalities in Italy. In her letters she tried to persuade the church authorities to return the papacy from Avignon to Rome. She also wrote to Pope Gregory XI himself, begging him to administer the Papal States. Throughout her life she composed about four hundred letters to kings, popes, cardinals, bishops, corporations and individuals.

On her return to Siena she founded a women's monastery, and at that time she produced her work entitled *Dialogue*. It was a work which was transcribed while Catherine was meditating: she would ask questions of the Higher Being she termed God and she received answers which were then written down as four treatises. The two main themes of this work are Mysticism and Union with God through love. The elements of Christian mysticism are described as being given in the first place by Divine Providence and of requiring Discretion, Prayer and Obedience. In the treatise on Discretion, Catherine dictated that love, humility and discretion are united. Discretion in penance is necessary, as the development of virtue is more important than paying penance. In the treatise on Prayer she describes how the soul proceeds from vocal to mental prayer and how prayer is a necessary activity to attain the pure and perfect love of God. This love of God should not be for one's own consolation but for one's neighbours and for the world. Our fellow human beings are the means whereby we find and strengthen our virtues. Regarding Obedience, God rewards those who are truly and promptly obedient because of their love for Him.

Catherine taught herself to write and eventually did not need scribes for her letters. The language used in the surviving letters is in high Italian and is said to be on a par with the writing of Petrarch in the classical Italian canon. Catherine also composed twenty-six prayers which are still highly respected today. In 1970 she was posthumously made a Doctor of the Church, the first woman to receive this honour, along with Teresa of Avila.

But Catherine was not destined to spend all her time immersed in writing, as a recluse. She was drawn again into the political arena and went back to Florence to try to bring about peace between that city and Rome. So full of conflict was the situation that an attempt was made on Catherine's life. However, peace was eventually agreed between these two warring factions in 1378. Catherine later went to Rome and remained for some time in the court of Pope Urban VI, where she supported his legitimacy and helped persuade various cardinals and members of the nobility to be loyal to him.

As her life went on Catherine ate less and less, until finally she received only the Holy Communion as daily sustenance. She described her inability to eat or keep food down without vomiting as an illness. From the beginning of 1380 she could no longer eat or drink and soon afterwards she was unable to walk. It was not very long before she had a stroke and died eight days later in April of that year, at the age of 33.

Because of her involvement in both religious and sectarian politics, and her peace campaigns in her own country, Catherine eventually became the Patron Saint of Italy along with Francis of Assisi. Centuries later, in 1999, she was named one of the six Patron Saints of Europe.

Catherine of Siena was a woman who had a remarkable

influence on world history and politics, in an age when women were generally dependent, untravelled and uneducated. Despite her infirmities she was, above all, driven by her mission to serve Christ in the world.

REVELATIONS
OF
DIVINE
LOVE

Margery Kempe

(*c.* 1378–after 1438)

In fourteenth-century England it was a man's prerogative to study and interpret the Bible or any other religious written work. Women were restricted to prayer and an inner, contemplative or emotional response to God. If a woman took vows to lead a religious life, she was not permitted to travel, even to a holy site, as this would inevitably lead to contact with men. However, Margery Kempe was a woman who defied these rules.

Because her behaviour fell outside the normal social boundaries of the time, Margery was considered by some to be insane. She had, in fact, suffered from serious post-natal depression before she made a total commitment to devote her life to Christ. This was an illness which was then misunderstood and for which there was no cure other than patience or, in serious cases, incarceration. After the birth of her first child, Margery's syndrome was so severe and potentially dangerous to herself and others that she was restrained and imprisoned for several months. It was Margery's darkest time, when she suffered from hallucinations of demons who tormented her and convinced her that she was a sinner. It was only when she had a vision of Christ, who told her that He had not forsaken her, that Margery became calm and eventually recovered.

A good marriage had been arranged for Margery, because she came from a privileged family, living in Norfolk. Her father was not only financially solvent but he also served as mayor. He represented his constituency in parliament, became a coroner and then a Justice of the Peace. Margery was set up with two domestic businesses, one brewing and the other corn-milling. Not only was she a business woman but Margery also went on to have fourteen children.

However, her experience of Christ changed her life forever. She continued to have visions, not only of Jesus but of Mary, God and some of the saints. She also had visions of herself as being present at the Holy Birth and at Christ's crucifixion She became extremely devout, going to church two, even three times a day, wearing a hair shirt. She was often heard to wail and plead forgiveness for her sins. Her weeping was very disturbing to others attending mass and she, too, found it disconcerting. Sometimes her visions were accompanied by sounds and strange, unknown perfumes. When she began to hear 'heavenly music' it moved her to tears. It was at this point that she decided to become celibate.

In Margery's day a wife or husband had to have their spouse's consent if they wished to enter a religious order, take vows of chastity, go on a pilgrimage or become a member of a Crusade. Eventually, Margery was able to negotiate a celibate marriage with her husband and they formalized their agreement in church. Her businesses had failed and, inspired by the Revelations of St Birgitta of Sweden, Margery was determined to go on a pilgrimage.

First, Margery went to consult the respected anchoress, Julian of Norwich, to ascertain the authenticity of her visions. She wanted to be sure that her reactions and her desire to travel for spiritual penance were well-founded. Julian confirmed that Margery's tears were a physical expression of her soul being filled with the Holy Spirit, and she did not denounce Margery's experiences. She advised her to listen to God rather than people's opinions and to continue to lead a life devoted to worshipping God and helping others.

Having gained confidence in her spiritual aspirations, Margery set off to obtain 'indulgences' (written pardons) for herself and for others, on a pilgrimage to the Holy Land. While on this pilgrimage she gave birth to her last child. She managed to live only on alms, travelling via Constance and Venice, where she remained for thirteen weeks, before reaching Jerusalem. She visited Calvary and, on her return journey, went to Assisi and then to Rome. Altogether, this pilgrimage lasted two years.

Two years later, Margery went on another long pilgrimage to Santiago de Compostela in Spain, following the route of St James. On her return she visited some holy sites in England, including the 'holy-blood shrine' in Hailes, Gloucestershire. In Leicester she was confronted by the church authorities and interrogated for illegal actions, as women were forbidden to preach. Margery insisted on being addressed in English rather than Latin, and defended herself competently. However, she was imprisoned for three weeks, having been accused of being a 'lying whore'. She returned to Lynn in Norfolk but continued to visit religious sites, shrines and individuals, such as the Archbishop of Canterbury.

Although Margery had come from a relatively privileged background, as she was a girl she had never been educated to read or write. She had learned the scriptures by heart and had heard various religious texts which were read to her. Over a period of more than forty years she dictated descriptions of her experiences, visions, visits to holy places, reflections and, above all, her 'conversations with Christ' in a work which became known as *The Book*.

The Book is considered to be the first autobiography written in the English language. It was lost for centuries until it was discovered in a private library in 1934. It became, and remains, a popular book for pilgrims and those seeking spiritual solace. (It was mentioned in a BBC documentary, *Pilgrimage*, in 2013.)

Although Margery was separated from her husband, when he became ill she went back to nurse him. Her son returned from Germany with his wife, in order to be with his father. Sadly, however, both he and Margery's husband died in 1431. She and her daughter-in-law journeyed back to Germany, where Margery visited more holy shrines, on her final pilgrimage.

It is not known when or where Margery died, but her legacy has lasted for six centuries. She was a wife and mother who found redemption and the restoration of her purity. Despite social, educational and physical limitations she travelled the world independently, gave spiritual advice to many and produced a Christian tract for many souls seeking an inner answer to their spiritual questions through the act of pilgrimage. Above all, Margery felt she had an intimate relationship with Christ, which gave her the strength and endurance to lead a life that was true to herself.

Teresa of Avila
(1515–1582)

Five hundred years ago a girl was born in Spain who, later in life, went on to develop her inner spiritual capacities as well as her intellectual ability. Her sense of community and strong will-forces helped to achieve the founding of a reformed Christian movement.

Teresa was born in the Avila region in 1515, to a Catholic mother and a father who had converted to Christianity, having bought his citizenship. Teresa's paternal grandfather was Jewish and had been persecuted by the Inquisition—later in her life, for different reasons, Teresa and her companions would also suffer accusations from the inquisitors. Because of their family history, Teresa's mother was anxious that her children be seen as pious Christians. To this end, she made various Christian publications available to her offspring, and Teresa avidly read about the lives of the saints. Having a strong imagination and a wilful sense of independence, Teresa, at the age of seven, persuaded her cousin to join her on an expedition to a community of Moors, whom she believed would behead them both, so rendering them Christian martyrs. Fortunately, the two children were spotted leaving through the gates of the city by their uncle and were returned home safely.

Sadly, Teresa's mother died when she was just 14. Teresa turned to the Virgin Mary to find solace through her prayers. Nevertheless, the emotional trauma of losing her mother as a young teenager must have contributed to her bad behaviour. She was, by all accounts, vain and flirtatious during this period. This caused her exasperated father to hand her over to the care of some Augustinian nuns. The measure was no doubt for disciplinary and educational reasons, and perhaps for convenience, rather than a step towards Teresa entering the convent as a novice. However, during her time with the nuns, Teresa read the preachings of St Jerome, and was so inspired by them that she decided to join a Carmelite order.

Teresa did not find her time in the convent easy: to pray in silence for any length of time she found almost impossible, as her intellectual mind was very active. It was only when she contracted malaria, which left her paralysed from the waist down for nearly three years, that Teresa was able to find the stillness required for meditative prayer. She read many tracts on spiritual exercises at this time, and came to see that the convent had fallen into a state of restlessness and frivolity. Many girls from wealthy families joined the convent and continued to enjoy a social life there. The rounds of visitors and chatter made it impossible to find the silence which Teresa had come to realize was necessary to communicate inwardly with Christ. She wrote:

'The first time our Lord bestowed upon me the grace of ecstasy, I heard these words: "I will not have thee converse with men but with angels."

Those words have been fulfilled; for [since then] I have never been able to form friendships with, nor have any comfort in, nor any particular love for, any persons whatever except those who, as I believe, love God and who try to serve Him.'

She decided that a reform of the Carmelite vows, particularly of poverty, was necessary, and with the help of a patron she founded a new convent. One of her principle aims was to help covert Spanish Jews to Christianity. By this time she was nearly 40 years old.

Teresa spent five years writing in seclusion, among other things forming a new 'Constitution' for the convent. She claimed she had visions of Jesus Christ throughout a two-year period, and during this time experienced a particularly life-changing sensation of being pierced by the Angel of Christ through her heart into her bowels, which caused an 'exquisite' pain. After this she focused on 'suffering with Christ' and was seen by the other nuns, on more than one occasion, to levitate during mass. Teresa was mortified that these effects of her spiritual exercises occurred in public and that she had, literally, to be held down by her companions. She explained this phenomenon:

A rapture is absolutely irresistible; whilst union, inasmuch as we are then on our own ground, may be hindered, though that resistance be painful and violent; it is, however, almost always possible. But rapture, for the most part, is irresistible. It comes, in general, as a shock, quick and sharp, before you can collect your thoughts, or help yourself in any way, and you see and feel it as a cloud, or a strong eagle rising upwards, and carrying you away on its wings.

I repeat it: you feel and see yourself carried away, you know not whither. For though we feel how delicious it is, yet the weakness of our nature makes us afraid at first , and we require a much more resolute and courageous spirit than in the precious states, in order to risk everything, come what may, and to abandon ourselves into the hands of God, and go willingly wither we are carried, seeing that we must be carried away, however painful it may be; and so trying is it, that I would very often resist, and exert all my strength, particularly at those times when the rapture was coming on me in public. I did so, too, very often when I was alone, because I was afraid of delusions. Occasionally I was able, by great efforts, to make a slight resistance; but afterwards I was worn out, like a person who had been contending with a strong giant; at other times it was impossible to resist at all: my soul was carried away, and almost always my head with it—I had no power over it—and now and then the whole body as well, so that it was lifted up from the ground.

Teresa was able to analyze and formulate her inner meditative work. She wrote about three levels of contemplation: the first was quiet recollection (picturing/ Imagination), the second she called 'Devotions of Silence', which allowed the spiritual world/God to speak to her as Inspiration, and the third she described as 'Devotions of Ecstasy or Total Union with God' (Intuition). In her writings she describes these states:

For if I say that I see Him neither with the eyes of the body, nor with those of the soul—because it was not an imaginary vision—how is it that I can understand and maintain that He stands beside me, and be more certain of it than if I saw Him? If it be supposed that it is as if a person were blind or in the dark, and therefore unable to see another who is close to him, the comparison is not exact. There is a certain likelihood about it, however, but not much, because the other senses tell him who is blind of that presence: he hears the other speak, or move, or he touches him; but in these visions there is nothing like this. The darkness is not felt; only He renders Himself present to the soul by a certain knowledge of Himself which is more clear than the sun. I do not mean that we now see either a sun or any brightness, only that there is a light not seen, which illumines the understanding so that the soul may have the fruition of so great a good. This vision brings with it great blessings.

It will be as well, I think, to explain these locutions of God... The words are very distinctly formed; but by the bodily ear they are not heard. They are, however, much more clearly understood than they would be if they were heard by the ear. It is impossible not to understand them, whatever resistance we may offer... There is another test more decisive: when our Lord speaks, it is at once word and work; and though the words are not meant to stir up our devotion, but are rather words of reproof, they dispose a soul at once, strengthen it, make it tender, give it light, console and calm it; and if it should be in dryness, or in trouble and uneasiness, all is removed, as if by the action of a hand, and even better; for it seems as if our Lord would have the soul understand that He is all-powerful and that His words are deeds.

In this state [of divine union] there is no sense of anything, only fruition, without understanding what that is the fruition of which is granted. It is understood that the fruition is of a certain good containing in itself all good together at once; but this good is not comprehended. The senses are all occupied in this fruition in such a way that not one of them is at liberty, so as to be able to attend to anything else, whether outward or inward.

Teresa's outer work consisted in establishing several other convents all over Spain and, in collaboration with John of the Cross and Anthony of Jesus, founding two Carmelite houses for men. Inevitably, her order and reforms began to come under the suspicion of the Inquisition and she was forced to retire. Only a relief from persecution, secured by King Phillip II of Spain, enabled her to continue her indefatigable work of writing and founding a new order of convents. In twenty years she founded more than thirty convents for nuns and cloisters for men.

Teresa was honoured with a doctorate-diploma for her books and was posthumously awarded the papal honour of Doctor of the Church in 1970, when, along with St Catherine of Siena, she was the first woman to be given this distinction. Her theologies were based on personal experience and, with her clear, analytical and perceptive abilities, she was able to explain the concept and practice of mystical Christianity to her readers.

Despite her heightened spiritual activities and achievements, Teresa was witty and practical. She often called for 'common sense' when dealing with conflictual situations and advised, above all else, that love was the essential factor, rather than rules, in any community. Her writings are didactic. She also wrote over five hundred letters giving advice to many people from different walks of life.

Teresa believed in the power of Holy Water in overcoming adversarial forces, and frequently spoke of mystical prayer as resembling water for the 'garden' of the soul:

> I am now speaking of the water which comes down from heaven to fill and saturate in abundance the whole of this garden with water. If our Lord never ceased to pour it down whenever it was necessary, the

gardener certainly would have plenty of rest; and if there were no winter, but an ever temperate season, fruits and flowers would never fail. The gardener would have his delight therein; but in this life that is impossible. We must always be careful, when one water fails, to obtain another. *This* water from heaven comes down very often when the gardener least expects it.[*]

[*]Ref: *The Life of Teresa Avila by Herself,* trans. by David Lewis (Digireads.com Publishing).

Mary Moffat

(1795–1871)

In the early 1800s a young English woman set sail for the African continent to marry the man she loved and become a Christian missionary. Despite many obstacles she spent half a century in Africa, practising her faith and spreading the Gospel in a way that made a deep impression on people there.

Mary Smith was born at the end of the eighteenth century in New Windsor. Her parents, James and Mary Smith, were devout Christians who instilled in her a strong moral code for life. Her father was Scottish and in the same year that Mary was born her future husband, Robert Moffat, was born in Scotland. Mary attended a Christian girls' school in Fairfield. When she was growing up, she supported her father's role as a seceder from the Providence Chapel by looking after the makeshift carpenter's shed which served as a temporary home for services. She cleaned, tidied, arranged hymn books and encouraged people to join the independent chapel.

Her father ran Dukinfield Nursery and a shop in Deansgate. His friend, Mr Roby, asked him to take on an apprentice who wanted to prove his ability to become a missionary. The young man, Robert Moffat, was duly hired and it was not long before love and a mutual ideal of converting people to Christianity drew Robert and Mary closely together. Mr Roby was delighted at the idea of Robert marrying Mary, who was a devout Christian with impeccable manners and the prospect of inheriting a small fortune.

However, Mary's parents strongly objected to her joining Robert as a missionary and forbade their relationship.

The pair were bitterly disappointed. Robert would marry no one else, so he sailed alone for Africa in 1816. He found the next year very trying, with no companion or help in a challenging and hostile environment. He had to rely on his faith in God, for during this time he received two letters from Mary, both of which reiterated her father's resolution not to consent to Mary's wish for marriage and a missionary life.

Two-and-a-half years passed before Mary's parents seemed to have a change of heart. They calmly stated they could no longer forbid her from following her own destiny, although they were heart-broken to let her go abroad, as she was their only daughter. Mary was also not without qualms and feared losing all that was dear to her—friends, family and country. But she knew from Robert's letters that he was suffering greatly without her. She assured her parents that their sacrifice for Christ would not go in vain, and sailed for Cape Town in 1819.

It was a dreadful journey for Mary, travelling alone. She suffered from illness and emotional grief until, at last, she met her future husband on African soil. They were married in St George's Chapel in Cape Town at the end of 1819. Mary was alarmed at how worn-out Robert looked, but soon they set off for their new station in Kuruman. Mary wrote to her parents that all was well and that she enjoyed wagon-life. She never complained of difficulties but was happy to be a missionary's wife, finally living and working in Africa. Undeterred by discomfort, she was content living in the vestry, which was a single room made of mud walls and floor.

It was not long, however, before she protracted a severe

illness which brought her to the brink of death. She feebly spoke her last wishes to her husband from her sick-bed. But, miraculously, she recovered and several months later gave birth to a baby daughter named Mary, who would later become the wife of David Livingstone.

Life in Kuruman was exceptionally hard because of the Botswanans' attitude towards the missionaries. They were not interested in hearing the Gospel, even after five years, and treated everything the Moffats did or owned with utter contempt. The missionaries had been granted some land which they cultivated, but this was systematically sabotaged, especially by the tribal chief's wife and tribeswomen. The women stole the corn, sheep, tools, as well as food and cooking utensils. Mary had to take items with her to the church services to prevent them from disappearing in her absence. The Botswanans never entered the small, makeshift church, and mocked any youngster who showed an interest in learning anything from the Moffats.

If Robert had to go away, Mary would always try to accompany him so that she could care for him, but inevitably there were times when she found herself alone in the face of solitude and danger. Her loneliness was at first due to the enormous rift between herself and the tribal Africans, who displayed a stubborn hatred towards her. One woman even threw a kitchen utensil at Mary's head while she was holding her baby. Through all of this ill-will, Mary prayed that Christ would help her and her husband to teach the natives the word of the Gospel. The Moffats were forced to leave Kuruman and take refuge elsewhere on more than one occasion, where Mary sometimes remained whilst Robert visited the interior of Africa on his missionary work. This was nerve-racking and frightening for Mary and the children. Their greatest threat at this time came from Chaka, a ruthless chief of the Matabele tribe. Mary was always greatly relieved whenever her husband returned home safely and they were together as a family once more.

On their return to Kuruman, the Botswanans, who were by now much depleted in numbers, began to accept the Moffats' constancy and determination. Their respect grew for them and the Moffats were able, in 1827, to have a stone house built to replace the wood-and-mud structure. One day, Mary pointed out to her husband that the Gospels were neither spoken or written in the local language, Sechwana. Although many native Africans could speak Dutch, Robert decided that the time had come for him to learn the language of the people. So he went to live with a tribe who only spoke Sechwana, and immersed himself in the language for several weeks. Despite this personal sacrifice of both husband and wife, Robert mastered Sechwana and, on his return home, started a school. He began by teaching four natives the Gospels in their own language. The school grew to provide lessons during both the day and evening, for nearly a hundred pupils. The hymns translated by Robert into Sechwana were very popular and made the school lessons enjoyable for everyone concerned.

Eventually, much to Mary's great joy, a communion service was held which was attended by a great crowd, many of whom were visibly and audibly moved. The strong, resistant Botswanans began to learn a new moral code based on the love of God.

In 1830 the Moffats purchased a printing press and managed to transport it to Kuruman, where Robert was able to print out the Bible and school lessons. He was now needed permanently at Kuruman to meet the growing demands of his missionary work. Mary had no choice but to travel alone to Cape Town to admit her children into school there, and also to receive treatment and rest for her own illnesses.

Robert had hoped that his translation of the New Testament would be printed in Cape Town but, as this was not possible, the Moffats decided to return to England for a prolonged visit. Mary was pregnant and gave birth to another daughter before they left the Cape. This event was mixed with sadness, for they lost their six-year-old son, James, who died of a measles epidemic on board ship.

Once in England, Robert Moffat was greeted with much interest and respect for his missionary work. He convinced David Livingstone, among others, of his destiny to become a missionary in Africa. Although Mary was happy to see her family and friends once more, by now she considered Kuruman to be her home and she longed to return to the place which she and her husband had worked so hard to transform. However, as Robert had a great deal of translating, printing, book-binding and dispatching to organize, the family did not set sail again for the Cape until 1843.

As they got nearer to Kuruman people flocked to greet them, for they were now welcomed and venerated by the Botswanans. For weeks after their return home, a stream of visitors came by. Their eldest daughter taught at the school until she, too, became the wife of a missionary, when she became Mrs David Livingstone. A tribal hunting party escorted Mary and her youngest to visit the Livingstones.

In 1847 Mary had to travel alone to Cape Town once more to take her younger children to school, a necessity which she always dreaded. All their lives, her children never forgot the care and loving kindness they received from their mother. One of Mary's sons, Robert, was only a baby when his father had visited the Mosilikatse tribe, which had a dreadful reputation. When he was 25-years-old, this son went as a missionary to the same warlike people but, sadly, died among them. It was only four months after the death of his sister, Mary Livingstone. Another son-in-law also died at Motito, adding to these tragedies in the Moffat family.

After fifty years as missionaries, Mary and Robert Moffat finally left Kuruman. They set off amid wailing crowds who thronged to bid them farewell, walking alongside their departing wagon as far as they were able. Six months later Mary caught a cold after their return to England, where she and her husband were honoured as retired missionaries. She died peacefully in 1871. Mary Moffat had suffered many trials for more than sixty years, which she bore through her profound faith and devotion to Christ.

Josephine Butler
(1828–1906)

Josephine Butler was not only deeply Christian but put her faith into practice as a radical social reformer. She campaigned tirelessly against the sexual abuse of women and children, in an age when it was unheard of for a woman to speak publicly of such matters.

She was born in 1828 in Northumberland as the seventh of ten children. Josephine had a largely happy childhood. Encouraged to learn art and music by her mother, she was particularly gifted on the piano. She also enjoyed dancing and riding. Horses remained a special love all her life. From her parents, rather than attendance at church, she learnt to live out the Christian principles in the gospels such as 'love thy neighbour' and to abide by passages in the Old Testament—for example, 'the oppressed should be freed' (Isaiah). Josephine's father was an exemplary landlord who provided his tenants with improved living and working conditions, better wages and an education for their children. He was also a Justice of the Peace and was instrumental in the abolition of slavery, the Catholic emancipation and the Reform Act of 1832. Josephine later wrote that she remembered her father shaking when he spoke of his abhorrence of slavery and Britain's part in it.

Josephine was distressed by the injustice and poverty that existed in society, particularly when she witnessed first hand people dying of hunger during her visit to Ireland. Later in her life she wrote that when she was 19 she had run into the woods to pray to God to have mercy on those who led a wretched existence.

Her passion against injustice was shared by her husband, George, whom she married when she was 24. He supported her work throughout her life. He was a kind, humorous, highly intelligent man who insisted their marriage should be 'a perfectly equal union'. George was deeply religious and was ordained as Bishop of Oxford in 1854. He was also a teacher in Oxford university. He and Josephine worked on a new version of Chaucer's poetry and studied Italian together within the academic environment where they spent their first years of marriage.

Josephine began to support the feminist movement and, in a truly Christian manner, opened her house to destitute women who were outcasts in the Oxford area. But by the time Josephine was expecting her third child, her health began to suffer and the family moved to better conditions in Cheltenham. But in their large Cheltenham house Josephine's fourth child, her only daughter Evangeline, tragically fell from the top stair banister and died at the age of five. For decades after, Josephine was haunted by the grief she felt. Her deep, largely private faith in Christ helped her through this terrible crisis. At the same time her compassion for other people's suffering grew. She became more determined than ever to do something about the plight of women and children in desperate circumstances.

When George was appointed headmaster of a boys' school in Liverpool, Josephine began to visit the inmates of Brownlow Hill Workhouse. This was a notorious institution which housed thousands of destitute souls, including many unmarried mothers and prostitutes. Josephine found homes for some of these women and invited them into her own home, particularly those who were nearing the end of their lives. She provided them with a safe environment and a dignified death.

Eventually, Josephine raised funds from wealthy sponsors to found her own refuge home for women. It was called the House of Rest and provided a means for women to earn an honest living, rather than turn to prostitution. Josephine gave these women a sense of self-worth; she was never moralizing as she was convinced that their plight had been unjustly brought upon them through unfair circumstances. It was not enough, Josephine realized, to merely be charitable or compassionate — women's civil and legal rights had to be improved.

So Josephine began to campaign for better education for women and for fairer wages. She pointed out that spinsters and widows were particularly vulnerable and could not be expected to receive smaller wages than men on the pretext that they were of 'childbearing age'. With the help of her husband and other teachers, she set up a series of courses for women in several towns in the north of England. The courses were on maths, science, literature, history and politics, and eventually hundreds of women joined the classes. Town libraries began to supply appropriate books for the academic edification of women who, until then, only ever considered that they would be wives and mothers. Josephine was elected President of the North of England Council for the Higher Education of Women. She was co-founder of this society with Anne Jemima Clough, who later became the principal of Newnham College, Cambridge, which Josephine was instrumental in establishing. At this time Josephine also began writing and published two articles, 'The Education and Employment of Women' and 'Woman's Work and Woman's Culture'.

These activities took their toll on Josephine's health and

she was forced to resign as President of the Council for Women's Higher Education. However, she then became involved in a campaign to repeal the Contagious Diseases Act of 1869. Her work with prostitutes had helped her to understand that these women were not the perpetrators of their demise, and that, rather than criminals, the contraction of sexually-transmitted diseases made them victims twice over. The Act declared that prostitutes should be subjected to genital examination by law or face imprisonment. If found to have an infection the women were incarcerated in hospital for three months. The whole process was intended to protect men, particularly in the Army and Navy, from contracting diseases through the services of prostitutes. It made the assumption that the women were entirely to blame and had to bear the consequences of behaviour instigated by men.

Josephine referred to these examinations as 'surgical rape' in her public speeches against the Act. It was offensive to many people in Victorian society for a woman to speak openly of such matters and on occasions Josephine was physically assaulted by those who opposed her. Nevertheless, she continued to campaign despite the dangers to herself and the jeopardy to her husband's career. George remained supportive and, although it took seventeen years, the Act was finally repealed in 1886.

Despite a gruelling regime—in one year alone she addressed ninety-nine meetings, four conferences and travelled 4,000 miles around England—Josephine felt her work was not finished with the repeal of the Contagious Diseases Act. A Ladies' National Association had been formed, books and pamphlets written and distributed, and two million signatures had been collected for a petition against the Act—methods later used by the suffrage movement. Josephine had also campaigned in Switzerland, France and Italy. It was on these visits that she became aware of the extent of child prostitution and a white slave trade on the Continent.

She persisted in making parliament and the public aware of the trade in young English girls, who were often kidnapped from their village homes, or tricked into becoming domestic servants in Europe, then groomed for sex and confined to a life in brothels. Even European royalty was guilty of perpetrating this activity on a large scale. Through Josephine's determination, the Criminal Law Amendment Act was pushed through in 1885 which raised the age of consent to 16 (as it stands today) and made it a criminal offence to procure girls for prostitution by threats, fraud or administering drugs.

When George was appointed canon of Winchester Cathedral, Josephine founded another House of Rest near Cathedral Close for friendless, betrayed, ruined women and girls. Not long afterwards George became ill and Josephine nursed him until his death. They had been married for thirty-eight years. Over the following two-year period, Josephine wrote a biography of George as a testament to the man and to their partnership. She found it too difficult to continue her work without George's support and, with her own health failing, continued writing letters until she died sixteen years later. There was no public funeral and she was buried in a small church in Northumberland. A newspaper wrote in her obituary: 'Mrs Butler's name will always rank amongst the noblest of those social reformers the fruit of whose labours is the highest inheritance that we have.'

Although Josephine was not interested in religious dogma or an allegiance to any particular church, she deeply venerated past Christian saints such as Teresa of Avila, Francis of Assisi and Catherine of Siena for their practice of inner prayer and devotion. Josephine herself 'prayed without ceasing' and retained this practice all her life—at times under tremendous strain from vilification and in the face of the hellish cruelty she witnessed in the world. She suffered without ever despairing because of her complete faith in Christ.

Today we should honour Josephine Butler and remember her work as we face the onslaught of global sex-slavery which uses sophisticated means such as computer technology, communications and transport. The rise in human trafficking has increased at an alarming rate and girls from poor backgrounds are lured to affluent countries such as Britain by the prospect of riches, fame or admiration, ending up as sexual objects paid minimally for the gratification of a huge, billion-dollar industry.

Josephine Butler once wrote: 'I appeal to Christ, and to Him alone, as the fountain-head of those essential and eternal truths which it is our duty and our wisdom to apply to all the changing circumstances of human society.' She also said: 'Do not imagine you are powerless ... God and one woman are a majority.'

Eglantyne Jebb
(1876–1928)

Eglantyne Jebb was an inspired and devoted humanitarian who, despite having no children of her own, founded the charity Save the Children, which is still operating more than a hundred years later.

Born into a ninteenth-century Shropshire landowning family as one of six children, Eglantyne enjoyed her early years exploring the countryside, riding ponies, catching butterflies and having picnics, as well as reading avidly. The freedom to roam the country environment as well as the household library gave her a sense of physical and intellectual independence, which remained with her all her life.

Eglantyne's parents were Anglican Conservatives with a strong social conscience, which they instilled in their off-spring. Her father, Arthur, was a considerate landlord to his tenants in Shropshire and Wales and often failed in his intentions to put the rent up, feeling that 'good hearts' were more valuable than money. He was also a barrister and expressed to his own children a great sense of satisfaction when, as one example, he won the acquittal of some young boys who had stolen a fishing-net. Her mother, also named Eglantyne, was a devoted parent. Nevertheless, she spread her energies to embrace other children who were less fortunate than her own.

One day, Eglantyne's mother came across a small boy who worked on their estate for six days a week, picking out stones from the fields. Mrs Jebb was determined to increase the prospects of the estate workers' children. She set up free classes for them in rural crafts such as wood-carving, chair-caning, basket-making, painting, mosaic-making and carpentry. Her own children joined in these workshops, which she administered as an institution called The Home Arts and Industries Association. Her vision was to have a network of women who would work with women's faith, love and hope to ensure that all children were given a bright future. 'Home Arts' attained national fame, instigating hundreds of classes all over the country; it even held annual exhibitions of rural crafts in the Royal Albert Hall, which were viewed by royalty.

From her mother and father, Eglantyne inherited a keen sense of social justice, a personal responsibility to society and an idealistic ambition. She was also influenced by a 'third parent', her Aunt Bun, who was less conventional than her own mother. Although strict about Eglantyne and her sisters' attending lessons, Bun believed that education should also take place outside the classroom. She often took the Jebb children on adventurous sallies to visit factories, castles and Roman ruins, on the bicycles which she had provided for them. Later, when the children were older, Aunt Bun supported their plans, whether for education or travel. She persuaded Eglantyne's parents that Eglantyne should fulfil her wish to attend Oxford and even paid for her undergraduate course.

Eglantyne, whose ambition had always been to become a writer, attended one of the two women's colleges at Oxford, Lady Margaret Hall. Having overcome her parents' resistance to her taking up an academic life, rather than marrying at the earliest opportunity, she read history and any books she could lay her hands on. At that time, women who undertook the same studies as men were not awarded a degree at the end of their undergraduate course. However, for Eglantyne the important thing was to learn as much as possible. She was very happy at university and joined the debating and drama societies. But sadly, not long after her father died, the death of her younger brother, Gamul, brought a tragic overtone to Eglantyne's life.

After Gamul's death, she joined the Catholic Apostolic sect, which respected personal spirituality and which she preferred to more organized churches. She became interested in mysticism and changed her course in order to make an independent study of the mystic practice in different faiths. She researched the Hindu Vedas texts, Greek stoicism and the visions of the eighteen-century mystic Jakob Böhme. Of her own modest experiences she said that to her 'spiritual awakening … is a feeling of oneness with humanity'. Eglantyne chose India as her final-year topic and always hoped to visit Asia. However, apart from one trip to Egypt, she never travelled outside Europe.

Eglantyne developed a spiritual connection with the dead, firstly in dreams about her brother Gamul, and then when she heard the voices of people who had died during the First World War, which she wrote about in her notes. She became interested in Spiritualism as well as religious mysticism, and for ten years kept a record of her transcendental experiences, including her vision of Christ's face. However, she did not have the confidence to lay much store by these experiences and was often assailed by feelings of failure and exhaustion. Nevertheless, she adhered to her own reasoning that 'if we lose our life, spending it for others, lavishing upon them our strength and our power, we find our life'.

Eglantyne had come to believe that 'heaven will grant willing hearts the means and opportunities of serving one's fellow men', and she was determined to fulfil a promise to her brother Gamul to make a difference to society. However, her Oxford education had neither afforded her a qualification nor any prospect of employment. Then she had the idea of becoming a teacher, under the auspices of the fairly recent legislation which directed compulsory education in Britain for all children up to the age of 12.

At the end of the nineteenth century, Eglantyne's ideals of education included the formation of individual character and the importance of practical work alongside academic achievement. She got a job as a teacher for underprivileged girls, having endured a teacher-training course for a year which required a great deal of patience and hard work, only serving to make her feel unworthy. She embarked on her teaching career, not out of enthusiasm or love for children, but out of a compulsion to serve society in some way. Inevitably, this ended in disaster but, more importantly, Eglantyne came to see that children's living conditions were absolutely fundamental to the efficacy of education.

From her experience of attempting to educate poor children, Eglantyne eventually started a relief fund for children in Europe who were affected by the First World War, called the Fight the Famine Council. Then she co-founded the Save the Children fund with her sister Dorothy, for which she campaigned and worked tirelessly. They produced pamphlets depicting starving children in England, Europe and Russia, which called for political intervention and financial help from the privileged classes. Her movement was often met with disdain and aggression but Eglantyne never wavered from her cause.

In 1922, Eglantyne drew up a five-point Charter for Children (the first of its kind) which she presented to the

Geneva International Union and which was later endorsed by the League of Nations. The points were as follows:

1. THE CHILD must be given the means requisite for its normal development, both materially and spiritually.
2. THE CHILD that is hungry must be fed; the child that is sick must be nursed; the child that is backward must be helped; the delinquent child must be reclaimed; and the orphan and waif must be sheltered and succoured.
3. THE CHILD must be the first to receive relief in times of distress.
4. THE CHILD must be in a position to earn a livelihood and must be protected against every form of exploitation.
5. THE CHILD must be brought up in the consciousness that its talents must be devoted to the service of its fellow-men.

This charter was the foundation of the later internationally renowned treaty for the universal rights of all children: the United Nations Convention on the Rights of the Child.

Eglantyne never married nor had children of her own. She had been disappointed in love and had lost the close friendship of a number of women who married and had families. The only children she felt personally connected to were her sister's and she never claimed to be fond of children in general. Her drive to bring the plight of children in need into the public consciousness was born out of a determination to help the humanitarian shortfalls in our civilization. Her work was also underpinned by her visions of Christ, which she believed to be a divine message of self-sacrifice. However, she did not find her life-mission an easy one, being prone to depression and suicidal thoughts as well as ill-health. The attempt to get sufficient funds for Save the Children was a constant challenge but, in her darkest moments, she continued to have a deep conviction that the movement would continue and find success.

Towards the end of her life she was hailed as an 'apostolic spirit' and was nicknamed 'the White Flame'. Her sister said of her that she was 'more spirit than flesh'; someone who aspired to living on a higher plane and who somehow kept herself alive by force of will alone. Yet Eglantyne recognized that children's bodies and minds require protection in a materialistic world.

Unaccountably, many people have never heard of Eglantyne Jebb—a woman who epitomized compassion for the young and innocent, instituted a fund for saving children's lives and wrote a policy of international and far-reaching importance, in an age when women had not yet even been given the right to vote.

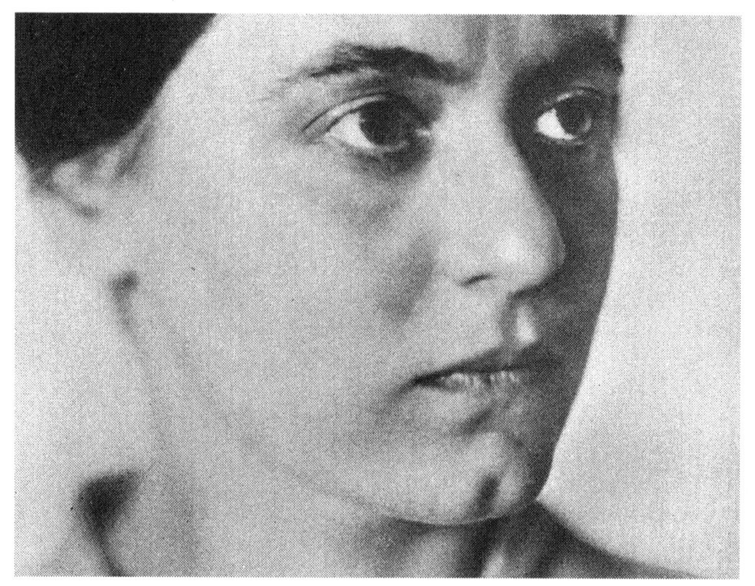

Edith Stein

(1891–1942)

Edith Stein was a brilliant academic, teacher, lecturer and suffragette, who converted from Judaism to Christianity and became a Carmelite nun. Her life ended tragically during World War Two, and she was canonized as St Teresa Benedicta of the Cross in 1998.

Edith was born in 1891 in Breslau, now called Wroclaw, in Poland. Twenty years earlier, Wilhelm of Prussia had become the Emperor of thirty-nine German-speaking countries and principalities, including Edith's family birthplace.

She was the youngest of eleven children in a Jewish family. Her grandmother and mother were both strong-willed, intelligent women and when Edith's father died her mother ably looked after both her large family and the family lumber business. Edith was especially close to her mother, having been born on the holiest day of the Jewish calendar, the Day of Atonement, Yom Kippur. As the youngest child, Edith was highly intelligent, precocious and quite an exhibitionist.

However, when she turned seven, Edith became more thoughtful and introverted. Her intellect developed rapidly but, at the same time, she began to feel more and more isolated and nervous. Even at this age she was intent on learning the truth about everything. She read avidly and was greatly relieved to go to school where she could study, ask questions and help others. Although she excelled, by the time she was 13 she had overtaxed herself. She decided to leave school and give help to her older, married sister and children.

This was a matter of consternation for her mother and teachers but Edith returned to her studies a few months later, more invigorated. During this new phase she delighted in learning Latin, and by the time she was 15 she was much loved and respected by her peers and siblings. However, secretly she began to lose faith in God although she never spoke of it, especially to her mother. Edith then decided to take up a career in teaching.

In 1911 Edith gained a place in Breslau University where she became interested in psychology and, importantly, phenomenology, under a professor named Edmund Husserl. Husserl blamed the current natural sciences for expounding that nature is entirely physical. He thought that this prevented human beings from searching for higher, spiritual values. This, he believed, had led to the decline of Western civilization. Professor Husserl set out to prove that science alone could not help people to understand the universe. His students were able to understand through rigorous, scientific thinking, the notion of 'Being'. Unintentionally, this led many of his students to an interest in Christianity.

Edith moved to Göttingen University to study under Professor Husserl and soon became his assistant. She also developed an interest in women's issues at this time, and joined the Prussian Association of Women's Suffrage. While Edith was committed to campaigning for equality for women, she nevertheless emphasized the different qualities inherent in women and men.

She still spent time with her mother in the synagogue, but a rift was forming between their beliefs. When Edith decided to do her doctorate dissertation on 'empathy' she met a fellow Jewish student who had converted to Catholicism. This idea was entirely new to Edith and she was further deeply influenced by a lecturer and his wife who had been baptised as Lutherans. The lecturer was Adolf Reinach, and Edith followed his example of volunteering to serve her country. She worked in an army hospital in Austria for some time before returning to her dissertation work at Freiburg University. Here she obtained her final degree with highest distinction.

When Adolf Reinach tragically died in Flanders, Edith was amazed at his widow's equanimity which she gained from her faith and hope in Christ. This was the determining factor in Edith's life, which convinced her of the power of Christianity.

She began studying the New Testament with what she described as a 'new spirit'. At about this time she was denied a professorship, not because she was unqualified, but because she was a woman. While staying with friends, Edith came across the autobiography of St Teresa of Avila. She read it avidly, deciding afterwards that this work was 'the truth' and a convincing thesis about God's love. The idea began to form in Edith's mind of becoming a Carmelite nun, following in St Teresa's footsteps. So she studied the Catechism and asked to be baptised into the Catholic Church. This was denied, until she demonstrated how quickly and thoroughly she had learned the required texts. She was baptised on New Year's Day, 1922, at the age of 31, taking her baptismal name of Teresa.

Edith began to attend Mass everyday. Sometimes she would slip out at dawn to go to church and then attend the synagogue later in the day with her mother, whom she could not bear to disappoint. Even more daunting was the idea of telling her mother that she desired to become a nun!

For the next eight years Edith taught at a Dominican school for girls, where she was loved and admired for her teaching ability and the way in which she practised her faith — as a living example of how one should respect one's fellow man or woman. She lived in the school as a Dominican sister and received no salary for her teaching work.

In 1925 she began translating several Catholic works and made a special study of St Thomas of Aquinas. Through studying his writings she realized that not only faith but reason and knowledge were necessary qualities on the path towards understanding God. For a while she spent time on a retreat in a Carmelite convent, where she was able to contemplate these ideas deeply. This had become necessary because Edith had been travelling extensively, lecturing about the role of women in modern society under the aegis of the Catholic church. She suggested that women would have to become more equal in the face of the dangers which she foresaw facing Germany. She had an insight into an approaching battle between good and evil and, in order to engage in this, she advised that education for girls was vital. Girls should be taught the same subjects as boys but the teaching method should be more suited to the natural, mediating characteristic inherent in women. During this time she was highly acclaimed as a lecturer but remained, in her words, a humble 'instrument of God'.

Despite excellent references and glowing reports, anti-semitism was gaining ground in Germany, so Edith was unable to obtain admittance as a professor at the universities of Freiburg or Breslau. She started work as a lecturer at the German Institute for Pedagogy in Münster having been, for the time being, dissuaded by fellow colleagues to pursue her wish to become a nun. In 1933 many

Jews lost their homes and businesses in Germany and Edith was asked to leave her position in Münster. However, at last she was able to fulfil her dream and, at the age of 42, Edith was accepted into the Carmelite convent in Cologne.

Her 84-year-old mother was resentful, but Edith would not now be swayed from her long-cherished desire. This was not without hardship, however, as Edith was no longer an admired academic and instead lived cloistered from the world, undertaking menial tasks. Her mother refused to communicate with her until her death. Nevertheless, Edith was overjoyed when her sister, Rosa, subsequently converted to Christianity.

Many academic friends and political fighters for women's rights attended Edith's 'clothing ceremony' at the convent, although no members of her family came. Probably because of the entourage of dignitaries at the ceremony, the Mother Superior asked Edith to finish her work of synthesizing the ideas of Thomas Aquinas with the phenomenology of Husserl. When Edith completed this it was entitled 'Act and Potency'.

Edmund Husserl converted to Christianity on his deathbed in 1938. That same year the Nazis launched Kristallnicht in Germany, destroying Jewish shops and synagogues and causing many Jews to flee the country. Edith was forced to go to a Carmelite convent in Holland for her own safety and that of her fellow sister-nuns in Cologne. She was now 47. Edith was content in the new convent and quietly resigned to whatever fate lay in store for her. Her sister, Rosa, was allowed to stay temporarily with her at the Dutch convent.

In 1940 Edith began work on the life of St John of the Cross, the contemporary of St Teresa of Avila, who wrote

The Dark Night of the Soul. That year the Nazis invaded Holland and Edith and Rosa began to receive warnings from the SS. Edith requested that she and Rosa might go to a convent in Switzerland. The Carmelite nuns in Switzerland said that they could take in Edith but not Rosa, who was not a nun. Edith sacrificed this opportunity by remaining with Rosa.

In 1942 all Jewish Catholics in Holland were rounded up. Some of Edith's siblings had already emigrated to America, but her brother and his family had recently been sent to a death-camp in Germany. On 2 August Edith and Rosa, among other Catholic nuns and priests, were herded to a detention centre, where family members were separated from one another. Edith comforted many of the women there and worked to keep the children clean and tidy. Survivors of the camp testified later that she always had a calm though sorrowful demeanour, and warmth of heart. She was able to get a parcel of blankets and toiletries from her former convent for the women and children, and she told the lorry driver that she believed she and Rosa were to be returned to their native Silesia.

But this was not the case. It was recorded that Edith and Rosa died in Auschwitz on 9 August, just one week after their capture. It is not clear exactly how they died but, in all likelihood, it was in the infamous gas chambers.

Sister Teresa Benedicta of the Cross believed in beginning a new search for Divine Truth each and every day. For her, there was a personal God who desires our friendship and love. She considered Mary, the mother of Jesus, to be the supreme example of motherhood, which encompasses the universal quality of caring for those in need. She is remembered for her support for the equality for women, her ideas on holistic education, her theological work and her work on empathy. She considered that empathy is a human quality whereby people communicate with one another silently, which she considered to be a vital element in community building.

Her path was the way of the cross, a path of suffering joyously undertaken for the world, in loving devotion to Christ. She was beatified as a martyr in 1987 and canonized in 1998 for the intercessory healing of a girl in intensive care who had swallowed a potentially lethal dose of paracetemol. The pediatric specialist in the Boston hospital said the girl's instant recovery was 'miraculous'.

Edith Stein, St Teresa Benedicta of the Cross, is one of the six patron saints of Europe.

Ita Wegman

(1876–1943)

At the turn of the twentieth century a young woman had an decisive role to play in Europe, where cultural, spiritual and scientific ideas were undergoing immense change.

Ita Wegman was born in West Java in Indonesia, which, in 1876, was still a Dutch colony. Her parents originated from Holland, her father working as a director of sugar plantations and manufacturing in the Dutch East Indies. When Ita was 15 she completed her childhood education in Europe and then returned to Java. She found life as a European colonial unsatisfactory, apart from the fact that she studied music under a teacher who led her to an interest in Theosophy. Eventually, due to ill health, her father was forced to retire and the family returned to Holland, where Ita undertook a training as a remedial gymnast and therapeutic masseur. While training, she visited the Theosophical Society in Haarlem, and when she went to Berlin to train in hydrotherapy she met Rudolf Steiner, who was then the General Secretary of the Theosophical Society in Germany. This was a life-changing meeting which determined Ita's destiny thereafter.

At the age of 26, while in Munich for a Theosophical Congress, Ita asked Rudolf Steiner if she could learn more from him. He invited her to his Esoteric Lessons and from this time onwards Ita regarded Steiner as her lifelong teacher. She became deeply interested in the new Christian movement based on his spiritual research, which was called Anthroposophy: a spiritual–philosophical study of the human being. Rudolf and his colleague, Marie von Sivers, convinced Ita to apply to a medical school to train as a doctor. At the time, Zurich University was the only nearby institution which accepted women, so Ita did her course there and obtained a medical diploma in 1911, specializing in gynaecology.

Ita went into private practice and after six years opened her own clinic in Zurich. Later she founded a specialist clinic in Arlesheim, where the medical indications of Rudolf Steiner could be put into practice. Here she developed a cancer treatment using extract of mistletoe, now called Iscador. This is an approved cancer treatment today in Germany and other countries, and is undergoing continued research in the USA.

She invited Rudolf Steiner to lecture in Switzerland many times and eventually the headquarters of the Anthroposophical Society was founded there. She and Rudolf Steiner researched a wide range of remedies, using the homeopathy method of extraction but incorporating mineral as well as plant essences. A complete medical course was developed by them over time. Their therapies included the use of injections, oils for massage and baths, remedial eurythmy, speech, art and counselling. The philosophy behind anthroposophical medicine was based on the spiritual knowledge of the whole person as a being consisting of physical body, soul and spirit. Where necessary, conventional intervention such as surgery was utilized, and a full medical training was compulsory for anthroposophical doctors. Above all, the knowledge that Christ is the great healer of humankind was the foundation for the study of anthroposophical medicine.

Ita Wegman also founded a therapeutic home for mentally-handicapped children, and the model for this is still upheld today. She co-founded a pharmaceutical company which grew healing plants and manufactured anthroposophical medicines. This company, named Weleda, still produces remedies and health-care products.

Ita supported many activities which arose out of Rudolf Steiner's research, including biodynamic farming and education, and she became a member of the Executive Council of the Anthroposophical Society at Rudolf Steiner's request. She and Steiner co-wrote a book on the medical knowledge which they had researched. In the last phase of Rudolf Steiner's terminal illness, Ita was constantly at his side as his doctor and nurse.

A central principle of Anthroposophy is the amalgamation of the tenets of reincarnation, karma and Christianity. It thus combines the esoteric knowledge of East and West. Through his ability to research the spiritual past of the earth's evolution and that of humanity, as well as of certain individuals, Rudolf Steiner understood that he and Ita Wegman had an important connection based on previous lives. On account of this they were able to work closely together for the future of humanity, particularly in the sphere of healing. Ita's understanding of this developed over time and she was encouraged by the exercises, meditations and verses which Steiner gave to her personally. One of the subjects of these meditative verses was the mythical persona of Persephone–Natura, who was banished to the Underworld from the sun-filled world above. Rudolf Steiner illustrated that, as a spiritual being, Persephone is sent by Christ, the Sun-God, to help mankind on earth and also to help the plant kingdom under the earth to serve the evolution of humanity. He indicated that, as a human soul, Ita Wegman's task and destiny was connected with this impulse. Furthermore, this spiritual impulse strives to understand the forces emanating from the cosmos and their connection with the elemental world. The Time-Spirit/Archangel of our age, Michael, has an overall responsibility for this. He hopes to bring humanity, out of free thinking and will, into the service of Christ and the future evolution of the earth. Ita Wegman lived and worked with this ideal as her main motivation.

After Steiner's death, Ita founded a new medical journal called *Natura*. In 1936, she extended her clinic in Ascona, Switzerland, which was near the headquarters of the Anthroposophical Society in Dornach. However, due to personality conflicts and differing viewpoints, Ita was asked to leave the Executive Council, and some of her supporters were asked to leave the Anthroposophical Society itself. Despite this, and perhaps motivated more strongly by it, Ita became devoted to promoting the work of Rudolf Steiner wherever possible and to extending a helping hand to any practical impulses which arose from his spiritual research. She was ill for a period of time but, after her recovery, she worked more intensively to understand Steiner's new spiritual-scientific ideas surrounding the event at Golgotha, Christ's Being and His importance for human beings and the whole of earth's evolution.

The conditions for continuing spiritual, anthroposophical work became very difficult due to the National Socialism which arose in Germany, followed by the Second World War. Ita spent some time in England and had a small circle of friends with whom she could share some of the knowledge she had gained through her close collaboration with Rudolf Steiner. She also developed her own abilities to research matters spiritually. She had been given meditative exercises to help develop her clairvoyant capacities in an appropriate, Christian manner, suitable for the modern person, by Rudolf Steiner himself. He had given similar exercises to others and Ita Wegman was sure that human beings would continue to develop their spiritual perception, despite the challenge of the materialistic thinking that mankind might otherwise extend throughout the world.

Ita was greatly inspired by the content of Rudolf Steiner's esoteric lessons, which formed the courses of a new 'mystery-school'. Even though she was excluded from the Society which Rudolf Steiner had himself inaugurated, Ita had faith in the foundation of it and remained hopeful that, in future lifetimes, the personal or karmic differences between its members would be overcome for the good of the earth and humanity.

She travelled extensively, giving lectures and continuing her work until she died in Arlesheim in 1943, at the age of 67. Ita Wegman's medical work continued to flourish and is still highly significant and widely practised today.

Evelyn Francis Capel
(1911–2000)

Rev. Evelyn Capel became the first woman priest of a new Christian movement in England in 1939. Born Evelyn Francis in Gloucestershire, she was educated in Cheltenham. She was one of five children, all girls, and attended a school for girls. Her father died when she was young so her mother had sole responsibility for Evelyn and her older sisters.

Evelyn was exceptionally intelligent and won the highest marks in England for the Oxford School Certificate, going on to win a scholarship to Somerville College, where she attained an Honours Degree in Modern History. The college tradition and Evelyn's family background were both Nonconformist. Graduates of Somerville (women's) College were reputed to be outspoken and forthright and Evelyn retained this characteristic all her life!

Evelyn had chosen to be a vegetarian at university. Notwithstanding, her first job was in Hammersmith, London, as a trainee manager for Lyons catering company. She worked in this commercial arena for nearly four years, during which time she was introduced to the spiritual research work of Rudolf Steiner. She studied his spiritual philosophy, Anthroposophy, avidly, and was drawn to emulate several people working in the different fields of practical application founded on it. She was particularly inspired by 'the best teacher of children I had ever come across' to become a 'Steiner teacher' herself. However, Evelyn eventually decided that she would rather serve every age-group, particularly adults who were searching for spiritual understanding. This motivated her to undertake the priests' training in the Christian Community in Stuttgart, which had been structured by Rudolf Steiner and some priests, and was undertaken in German. So, before she could embark on the training she had to learn the German language.

Women were never excluded from becoming priests from the very foundation of the Christian Community, although very few actually took up the possibility. Evelyn was ordained in 1939 at the age of 28, becoming the first Christian Community woman priest in Britain. As such, she was also the first woman priest to celebrate the Transubstantiation and Eucharist in Britain. Six years later, she was the Community Representative at the ordination of the first woman priest in Holland. Many women were ordained in this religious movement in the years to follow.

The Christian Community was first named the Movement of Religious Renewal, and was founded by a group of priests and trainee priests in Germany, with guidance and advice from Rudolf Steiner. Having been inaugurated in 1922, it was still a young movement of which Evelyn Francis was one of its pioneers. This pioneering spirit remained throughout her career.

Evelyn was fortunate to get out of Germany via Holland at the start of the Second World War. During the war the priests of The Christian Community in Germany had to flee for safety from the Nazi regime, and one of the founders, Dr Alfred Heidenreich, came to England. Here he was able to translate the sacramental texts of The Christian Community into English and become the church leader in Britain. However, as he was not permitted to travel, Evelyn represented the community for him in Germany and other

European countries on several occasions. She travelled as a colonel of the Religious Affairs Department of the Allied Control Commission for Germany in order to re-group and stabilize various dispersed congregations, once the war was ended.

In her autobiographical book *A Woman in the Priesthood* Evelyn Francis Capel describes how women throughout history have provided inspiration from the heavenly world of angelic beings and have been accepted as saints, albeit generally withdrawn from worldly matters. She also mentions the important part abbesses have played in history in regulating and ordering religious life, providing a space for spiritual enquiry and development and making sanctuaries and healing environments available for all. However, carrying out religious ceremonies as priests has never been advocated—this is a sphere of work which has only become acceptable in our modern era, as now both men and women have developed an 'I' or ego-consciousness.

Evelyn worked as a priest in London and felt that the city should be the centre of her service, which could then ray out to other parts of the world. That caused some conflict with the church-leaders, as she refused to leave what she had established in the way of a congregation and church-building. Eventually, Evelyn set up a Christian Community base in Hammersmith, West London, with a chapel for sacramental services, accommodation, space for conferences and study groups, a garden and a small publishing house. She wrote many articles and books, gave lectures and provided counselling, with remarkable clarity of thought and compassion. She also supported a local adult education institute and became a Fellow of the Royal Society of Arts in London.

Evelyn's first husband had died before the West London base was established. One day Evelyn met a London cab-driver, whom she later married. Bert Capel was a devout Christian who assisted her greatly in the running of the centre.

As well as her duties in London, Evelyn supported the Christian Community as a world movement and became one of is pioneers in Europe, Africa, Australia and the USA. In the 1960s she went to Africa for a holiday but ended up working there, eventually instigating the founding of the Christian Community in South Africa. She visited Africa over a period of more than thirty years to baptise, confirm, hold services, give lectures, advise and support ventures in towns and farms. Many of these places were widely dispersed and isolated; she visited Cape Town, Pretoria, Johannesburg, Harare, farms in Zimbabwe and Accra in Ghana.

As a working priest for over fifty years she supported the celebration of the Christian sacraments in Germany, Austria, Holland, Switzerland, Poland, Portugal and on the African, American and Australian continents. In certain circumstances she was not averse to holding a sacramental service, such as a baptism, in a garden, room of a house, or even on a Welsh mountain! She often travelled long distances in the face of possible danger and experienced considerable discomfort. Undaunted, she felt she should never refuse anyone who asked for any of the sacraments.

Evelyn Capel had the courage to overcome obstacles and defy convention. She grasped the opportunities which were presented to her, for example to be ordained as a priest and to travel around the world as a church ambassador. She put her intellect, education, keen interest in the arts and profound understanding of the spiritual-scientific research of Anthroposophy to good use, in her writing, lectures and discussions. Socially, her centre was open to all and she welcomed people from all over the world who came to visit. She was always available to give counsel or advice and to encourage people to experience the services of the Christian Community. The sacramental services remained the most important *raison d'être* for every task she undertook.

After her husband Bert died, Evelyn found it more and more difficult to run the centre, although she was determined to continue the work there. She was reluctant to retire as a priest and only did so after considerable persuasion. Other priests took over her duties and the centre is still thriving today, having recently opened a new chapel there. The Christian Community continues to celebrate the sacraments worldwide.

Evelyn Francis Capel died peacefully in Kent on 5 January 2000, at the age of 89.

Conclusion:
CONTEMPLATING THE ETERNAL FEMININE

Christ formed a brotherhood of disciples and we have evidence that some of these men travelled far and wide to teach and heal in His name. Their activity was in the sphere of *space*. There were also some female members of the community around Christ but their significance had to do with future *time*. A clue to this lies in the mystery of Christ's proclamation to Martha: I AM the Resurrection and the Life.

Martha and her sister Mary (Magdalene) played an important part in Christ's life, for we read in John 11:5 that 'Christ loved Martha and her sister and Lazarus'. These two ordinary women were healed by Christ and, more importantly, they became prototypes for a future humanity which will wholly unite with Him. Already, this future possibility is beginning to be a reality in our own time as we strive, through inner work, to receive the Christ into our own ego-vessels and thereby unite with our higher selves.

The tremendous proclamation with its infinite power, which was bestowed upon Martha in the I AM saying, awakened in a human being the awareness that Christ would overcome death and continue to live in all future time. The understanding of this was absorbed by Mary from Martha through the closeness of the two sisters.

The proclamation was then proven to Mary Magdalene, who was the first to recognize the Risen Christ. She was given the task to prepare others to recognize Him. Christ gave Mary the instruction: 'Now go to my brothers and say to them: I ascend to my Father who gives existence to me and to you and who lives as a divine power in me and also in you.'

Mary prepared the disciples with what she had been told by the Lord, and a few hours later (the evening of that day) the disciples recognized Christ when he appeared among them in the locked room. He showed them his hands and side as a signifier, blessed them and gave them their mission, through the power of the Holy Spirit, to release others of sin.

He gave many other signs, for example to Thomas, and to the other disciples. John wrote some of these down to give humanity the power of faith in Christ's name. The disciple whom Jesus loved recognized the Risen Lord standing on the shore of the Sea of Tiberias, and the other disciples recognized Him when He shared a meal of bread and fish with them. After Mary had told 'those who walked with Jesus' that she had seen the Risen One who lives, Christ revealed himself to 'two others on the way as they were walking over the fields' (Mark 16).

On the day of the Resurrection, Cleopas and another person were accompanied by a stranger on the road to Emmaus. They told the stranger that some women of their circle had found Christ's body missing from the tomb. A vision of angels had told the women that Jesus, who had been crucified, now lived. With this news uppermost in their minds, although they did not recognize Him at first, the two perceived that the stranger was Christ when he broke the bread and gave it to them to eat. The message which had been broadcast by the women came to light for a moment, in a vision which the two men beheld, before it vanished again.

When these two returned to Jerusalem, they were told that the Lord had also been perceived by Simon. Christ then appeared in the midst of the group and ate fish before their eyes. Finally, He appeared to the eleven disciples and gave them their apostolic mission before his Being grew wide, expanding into the atmosphere, and He disappeared from sight. So the proclamation to Martha, 'I am the Resurrection', was fulfilled. The experience of this was reiterated at Whitsun and later by Paul on the road to Damascus. It is experienced by some today and will be experienced by more people as time goes on.

But what of the second part of the proclamation to Martha — 'I AM the Life'? This means the life which overcame death, bringing about the Resurrection. It refers to the life forces of the earth which are renewed by Christ and also to the life-to-come. We can be sure it means all of these things, but the mystery remains regarding the fact that this was proclaimed to a seemingly insignificant person: Martha.

We read clearly in the Gospels of the mention made merely of 'some women' who accompanied Jesus. Among the disciples there are no women — certainly not among the twelve. So those who are named stand out in particular relief and perhaps are all the more significant because of it.

Of course, the culture in which Christ Jesus lived held a different view of women than ours today. In the ancient Greek civilization women were itemized as part of the chattel belonging to a man, along with animals and furniture! However, men had a duty to protect and provide for the women in their families. In the Jewish tradition too, women were well guarded by the men as they were the child-bearers who continued the blood-line of the Jewish people. Apart from the important tasks of raising children and giving support to husbands, in the centuries after Christ walked the earth a few exceptional women, through their faith in Him, achieved physical, emotional and intellectual independence. They made a difference to the history of Western civilization and the morality of human society (see Part Two).

But the idea of legal, political, financial and social equality for all women is only very recent in our history — in its infancy, in fact. Long after African-Americans in the USA were given the right to vote, the privilege was granted to women. Since then there have been wave upon wave of feminist movements, working to bring an awareness of the discrepancies between men and women in the workplace, of injustice, abuse and slavery of women on a global scale. The fight for the equality of women is the first outward sign that the feminine side of the human psyche must be acknowledged and developed. The inner reason is that this development is hugely important for the future progress of humanity.

The prophetic, apocalyptic Book of Revelation by John describes, in pictures and esoteric symbols, the future development of human beings and the earth. Three particular images are highlighted which have a feminine quality — the Woman clothed with the Sun, the Whore of Babylon and the Bride.

The woman enveloped by the cosmic forces of the moon, sun and stars symbolizes the young universal soul from which the higher human being will eventually develop (pictured as the child waiting to be born). However, the higher ego must be incorporated by the free activity of the human being, and this is a process fraught with danger (symbolized by the dragon). Martha represents the young, naïve soul (she complains, like a little girl, that she has to do more work than her sister) who, through many incarnations over ages of time, will develop the capacity to unite with her spiritual, higher ego. The image of the child taken up to heaven shows us the higher ego of humanity which remains discarnated until, through the indwelling of the Christ Being in the human soul and spirit, it is able to incarnate as the new Spirit Man. The unity of the mature, Christ-filled soul with its higher ego, which is of the same essence as the being of Christ, is described in Revelations as the marriage of the bride with the Lamb.

The Whore is also connected with something having the semblance of a lamb, but which is actually the Beast. There is no marriage between the Whore and the Beast because the old, outmoded soul-aspect of the Whore uses the hardened body and resources of the earth like a slave (a Beast of burden) for her own aggrandisement. The glittering jewellery she wears represents everything that can be taken from the material world: everything that can be manufactured from its substance and all the thinking and will forces which are bound up with this.

The word 'whore' has come to mean a woman who offers sex for money, devoid of love or relationship. Whoring once had another meaning, which is 'idolizing'. Eventually, the 'Slave-Beast' will turn against the 'idolatrous' soul in hatred, and both parties, that is the depleted earth and the de-humanized population, will destroy one another — according to John's Revelations.

The part of the soul which remains pure in the love of the Christ Being will understand the necessity of casting out the unhealthy 'canker' within it, in order to remain healthy and alive. In fact, the soul becomes all the more suitable as a vessel for the spirit on account of the suffering which it has to undergo in the battle with the double evil of the

Whore and the Beast—somewhat like the pearl which is formed by the grit within the oyster shell. That part of the soul which is the ego bearer becomes appropriately available to receive its higher ego, united with the Christ. The unredeemed portion of humanity and the untransformed part of the earth will, in the final analysis, fall away.

As human beings become ever more perfected through repeated incarnations, they will be sufficiently prepared to 'attend the wedding' of the marriage between the Being of Christ and the Earth—which also becomes transformed into its higher, spiritual state. Through the efforts of a number of human beings to align themselves completely with Christ over the ages, a 'New Jerusalem' will be formed, which will continue to exist and advance into the future. This New Jerusalem is also said to be like a bride adorned for marriage—it is the prototype of the future humanity come to fruition in union with Christ, who will continue to lead the evolution of our planet.

During Christ's incarnation on earth He found the heart forces of women servants to be more fertile 'ground' in which to plant the seed of a new humanity than that, for example, of the Scribes and Pharisees. This gives us a moral indication that both men and women today need consciously to develop the higher feminine soul attributes of service, devotion, empathy and love. These qualities should accompany our knowledge about the spiritual world: the true wisdom or 'Sophia'.

The Archangel Michael affords the possibility of this knowledge becoming part of mankind's consciousness, along with the courage we need to fight, as 'golden warriors', for an eternal world.

In the last chapter of the Revelation to John, reference is made to the Life, which was first spoken of to Martha:

'Only he can gain entrance into the New Jerusalem whose name is written in the Book of Life which belongs to the Lamb.' Christ, who released the necessary forces at the beginning of the Creation by 'opening the book' (Revelation 5) ensures renewed life to those who remain, are or become united with Him.

'And the Spirit and the bride say, Come! And he who hears this call let him also say, Come! Let him who is thirsty come. Let him who desires freely drink of the Water of Life!' The united masculine, spiritual element and feminine, higher-soul element of the future human being does not take, but gives, an invitation to all those who wish to share in the community of eternal Life.

Bibliography

Emil Bock, *The Childhood of Jesus*, Floris Books, 1997

Evelyn Francis Capel, *The Christian Year*, Floris Books, 2012
The Spirit Within Us, Floris Books, 2010
A Woman in the Priesthood, Temple Lodge Publishing, 1992

Anne Katherine Emmerich, *Dolorous Passion of Our Lord Jesus Christ*, T A N Books & Publishers, 1994

Rod Garner, *Josephine Butler, A Guide to her Life, Faith and Social Action*, Darton Longman and Todd, 2009

Ed. Rudolf Kirst, *Evelyn Francis Capel, A Celebration of a Pioneering Spirit*, Temple Lodge Publishing, 1997

David Lewis, *The Life of Teresa Avila by Herself,* Digireads.com Publishing, 2009

Bernard Lievegoed, *Phases*, Rudolf Steiner Press, 1998

Clare Mulley, *The Woman Who Saved Children*, Oneworld Publications, 2010

Rudolf Steiner, *Occult Science*, Rudolf Steiner Press, 2013
The Fifth Gospel, Rudolf Steiner Press, 1998
Karmic Relationships Vol. IV, Rudolf Steiner Press, 1997 (for indications about Hrotsvite)

Alex Terego, *Edith Stein, Philosopher, Mystic, Martyr, Feminist*, Kindle edition, 2013